Quantitative Methods for the Social Sciences

Daniel Stockemer

Quantitative Methods for the Social Sciences

A Practical Introduction with Examples in SPSS and Stata

 Springer

Daniel Stockemer
University of Ottawa
School of Political Studies
Ottawa, Ontario, Canada

ISBN 978-3-319-99117-7   ISBN 978-3-319-99118-4   (eBook)
https://doi.org/10.1007/978-3-319-99118-4

Library of Congress Control Number: 2018957702

This Springer imprint is published by the registered company Springer Nature Switzerland AG
The registered company address is: Gewerbestrasse 11, 6330 Cham, Switzerland

Contents

Under what conditions do countries go to war? What is the influence of the 2008–2009 economic crisis on the vote share of radical right-wing parties in Western Europe? What type of people are the most likely to protest and partake in demonstrations? How has the urban squatters' movement developed in South Africa after apartheid? There is hardly any field in the social sciences that asks as many research questions as political science. Questions scholars are interested in can be specific and reduced to one event (e.g., the development of the urban squatter's movement in South Africa post-apartheid) or general and systemic such as the occurrence of war and peace. Whether general or specific, what all empirical research questions have in common is the necessity to use adequate research methods to answer them. For example, to effectively evaluate the influence of the economic downturn in 2008–2009 on the radical right-wing success in the elections preceding the crisis, we need data on the radical right-wing vote before and after the crisis, a clearly defined operationalization of the crisis and data on confounding factors such as immigration, crime, and corruption. Through appropriate modeling techniques (i.e., multiple regression analysis on macro-level data), we can then assess the absolute and relative influence of the economic crisis on the radical right-wing vote share.

Research methods are the "bread and butter" of empirical political science. They are the tools that allow researchers to conduct research and detect empirical regularities, causal chains, and explanations of political and social phenomena. To use a practical analogy, a political scientist needs to have a toolkit of research methods at his or her disposal to build good empirical research in the same way as a mason must have certain tools to build a house. It is indispensable for a mason to not only have some rather simple tools (e.g., a hammer) but also some more sophisticated tools such as a mixer or crane. The same applies for a political scientist. Ideally, he or she should have some easy tools (such as descriptive statistics or means testing) at his or her disposal but also some more complex tools such as pooled time series analysis or maximum likelihood estimation. Having these tools allows

© Springer International Publishing AG 2019
D. Stockemer, *Quantitative Methods for the Social Sciences*,
https://doi.org/10.1007/978-3-319-99118-4_1

political scientists to both conduct their own research and judge and evaluate other peoples' work. This book will provide a first simple toolkit in the area of quantitative methods, survey research, and statistics.

There is one caveat in methods training: research methods can hardly be learnt by just reading articles and books. Rather, they need to be learnt in an applied fashion. Similar to the mixture of theoretical and practical training a mason acquires during her apprenticeship, political science students should be introduced to methods' training in a practical manner. In particular, this applies to quantitative methods and survey research. Aware that methods learning can only be fruitful if students learn to apply their theoretical skills in real-world scenarios, I have constructed this book on survey research and quantitative methods in a very practical fashion.

Through my own experience as a professor of introductory courses into quantitative method, I have learnt over and over again that students only enjoy these classes if they see the applicability of the techniques they learn. This book follows the structure as laid down in Fig. 1.1; it is structured so that students learn various statistical techniques while using their own data. It does not require students to have taken prior methods classes. To lay some theoretical groundwork, the first chapter starts with an introduction into the nuts and bolts of empirical social sciences (see Chap. 2). The book then shortly introduces students to the nuts and bolts of survey research (see Chap. 3). The following chapter then very briefly teaches students how they can construct and administer their own survey. At the end of Chap. 4, students also learn how to construct their own questionnaire. The fifth chapter, entitled "Conducting a Survey," instructs students on how to conduct a survey in the field. During this chapter, groups of students test their survey in an empirical setting by soliciting answers from peers. Chapters 6 to 9 are then dedicated to analyzing the survey. In more detail, students learn how to input their responses into either an SPSS or STATA dataset in the first part of Chap. 6. The second part covers univariate statistics and graphical representations of the data. In Chap. 7, I introduce different forms of means testing, and Chap. 8 is then dedicated to bivariate correlation and regression analysis. Finally, Chap. 9 covers multivariate regression analysis).

The book can be used as a self-teaching device. In this case, students should redo the exercises with the data provided. In a second step, they should conduct all the tests with other data they have at their disposal. The book is also the perfect accompanying textbook for an introductory class to survey research and statistics. In the latter case, there is a built-in semester-long group exercise, which enhances the learning process. In the semester-long group work that follows the sequence of the book, students are asked to conceive, conduct, and analyze survey. The survey that is analyzed throughout is a colloquial survey that measures the amount of money students spend partying. Actually, the survey is an original survey including the original data, which one of my student groups collected during their semester-long project. Using this "colloquial" survey, the students in this study group had lots of fun collecting and analyzing their data, showing that learning statistics can (and should) be fun. I hope that the readers and users of this book experience the same joy in their first encounter with quantitative methods.

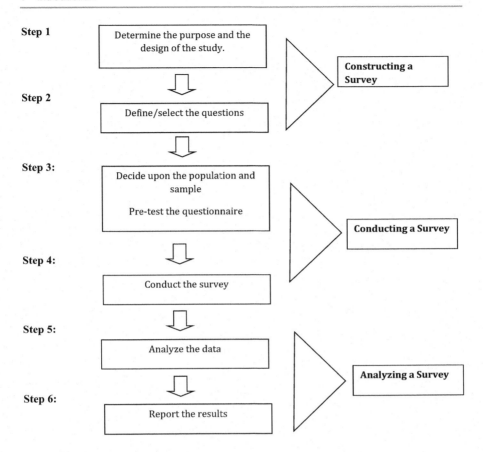

Step 1

Determine the purpose and the design of the study.

Constructing a Survey

Step 2

Define/select the questions

Step 3:

Decide upon the population and sample

Pre-test the questionnaire

Conducting a Survey

Step 4:

Conduct the survey

Step 5:

Analyze the data

Analyzing a Survey

Step 6:

Report the results

Fig. 1.1 Different steps in survey research

The Nuts and Bolts of Empirical Social Science

2

Abstract

This chapter covers the nuts and bolts of empirical political science. It gives an introduction into empirical research in the social sciences and statistics; explains the notion of concepts, theories, and hypotheses; as well as introduces students to the different steps in the quantitative research process.

2.1 What Is Empirical Research in the Social Sciences?

Regardless of the social science sub-discipline, empirical research in the social sciences tries to decipher how the world works around us. Be it development studies, economics, sociology, political science, or geography, just to name a few disciplines, researchers try to explain how some part of how the world is structured. For example, political scientists try to answer why some people vote, while others abstain from casting a ballot. Scholars in developmental studies might look at the influence of foreign aid on economic growth in the receiving country. Researchers in the field of education studies might examine how the size of a school class impacts the learning outcomes of high school students, and economists might be interested in the effect of raising the minimum wage on job growth. Regardless of the discipline they are in, social science researchers try to explain the behavior of individuals such as voters, protesters, and students; the behavior of groups such as political parties, companies, or social movement organizations; or the behavior of macro-level units such as countries.

While the tools taught in this book are applicable to all social science disciplines, I mainly cover examples from empirical political science, because this is the discipline in which I teach and research. In all social sciences and in political science, more generally, knowledge acquisition can be both normative and empirical. Normative political science asks the question of how the world ought to be. For example, normative democratic theorists quibble with the question of what a democracy ought

© Springer International Publishing AG 2019

D. Stockemer, *Quantitative Methods for the Social Sciences*,

https://doi.org/10.1007/978-3-319-99118-4_2

to be. Is it an entity that allows free, fair, and regular elections, which, in the democracy literature, is referred to as the "minimum definition of democracy" (Bogaards 2007)? Or must a country, in addition to having a fair electoral process, grant a variety of political rights (e.g., freedom of religion, freedom of assembly), social rights (e.g., the right to health care and housing), and economic rights (e.g., the right to education or housing) to be "truly" democratic? This more encompassing definition is currently referred to in the literature as the "maximum definition of democracy" (Beetham 1999). While normative and empirically oriented research have fundamentally different goals, they are nevertheless complementary. To highlight, an empirical democracy researcher must have a benchmark when she defines and codes a country as a democracy or nondemocracy. This benchmark can only be established through normative means. Normative political science must establish the "gold standard" against which empirically oriented political scientists can empirically test whether a country is a democracy or not.

As such, empirical political science is less interested in what a democracy should be, but rather how a democracy behaves in the real world. For instance, an empirical researcher could ask the following questions: Do democracies have more women's representation in parliament than nondemocracies? Do democracies have less military spending than autocracies or hybrid regimes? Is the history curriculum in high schools different in democracies than in other regimes? Does a democracy spend more on social services than an autocracy? Answering these questions requires observation and empirical data. Whether it is collected at the individual level through interviews or surveys, at the meso-level through, for example, membership data of parties or social movements, or at the macro level through government/international agencies or statistical offices, the collected data should be of high quality. Ideally, the measurement and data collection process of any study should be clearly laid down by the researcher, so that others can replicate the same study. After all, it is our goal to gain intersubjective knowledge. Intersubjective means that if two individuals would engage in the same data collection process and would conduct the same empirical study, their results would be analogous. To be as intersubjective or "facts based" as possible, empirical political science should abide by the following criteria:

Falsifiability The falsifiability paradigm implies that statements or hypotheses can be proven or refuted. For example, the statement that democracies do not go to war with each other can be tested empirically. After defining what war and democracy is, we can get data that fits our definition for a country's regime type from a trusted source like the *Polity IV* data verse and data for conflict/war from another high-quality source such as the *UCDP/PRIO Armed Conflict* dataset. In second stop, we can then use statistics to test whether the statement that democracies refrain from engaging in warfare with each other is true or not.[1,2]

Transmissibility The process through which the transmissibility of research findings is achieved is called replication. Replication refers to the process by which prior findings can be retested. Retesting can involve either the same data or new data from the same empirical referents. For instance, the "law-like" statement that democracies do not go to war with each other could be retested every 5 years with the most recent data from *Polity IV* and the *UCDP/PRIO Armed Conflict* dataset covering these 5 years to see if it still holds. Replication involves high scientific standards; it is only possible to replicate a study if the data collection, the data source, and the analytical tools are clearly explained and laid down in any piece of research. The replicator should then also use these same data and methods for her replication study.

Cumulative Nature of Knowledge Empirical scientific knowledge is cumulative. This entails that substantive findings and research methods are based upon prior knowledge. In short, researchers do not start from scratch or intuition when engaging in a research project. Rather, they try to confirm, amend, broaden, or build upon prior research and knowledge. For example, the statement that democracies avoid war with each other had been confirmed and reconfirmed many times in the 1980s, 1990s, and 2000s (see Russett 1994; De Mesquita et al. 1999). After confirming that the *Democratic Peace Theory* in its initial form is solid, researchers tried to broaden the democratic peace paradigm and examined, for example, if countries that share the same economic system (e.g., neoliberalism) also do not go to war with each other. Yet, for the latter relationship, tests and retests have shown that the empirical linkage for the economic system's peace is less strong than the democratic peace statement (Chandler 2010). The same applies to another possible expansion, which looks at if democracies, in general, are less likely to go to war than nondemocracies. Here again the empirical evidence is negative or inconclusive at best (Daase 2006; Mansfield and Snyder 2007).

Generalizability In empirical social science, we are interested in general rather than specific explanations; we are interested in boundaries or limitations of empirical statements. Does an empirical statement only apply to a single case (e.g., does it only explain why the United States and Canada have never gone to war), or can it be generalized to explain many cases (e.g., does it explain why all pairs of democracies don't go to war?) In other words, if it can be generalized, does the democratic peace

---

[1]The Polity IV database adheres to rather minimal definition of democracy. In essence, the database gauges the fairness and competitiveness of the elections and the electoral process on a scale from -10 to $+10$. -10 describes the "worst" autocracy, while 10 describes a country that fully respects free, fair, and competitive elections (Marshall et al. 2011).

[2]The UCDP/PRIO Armed Conflict Dataset defines minor wars by a death toll between 25 and 1000 people and major wars by a death toll of 1000 people and above (see Gleditsch 2002).

paradigm apply to all democracies, or only to neoliberal democracies, and does it apply across all (normative) definitions of democracies, as well as all time periods?). Stated differently, we are interested in the number of cases in which the statement is applicable. Of course, the broader the applicability of an explanation, the more weight it carries. In political science the Democratic Peace Theory is among the theories with the broadest applicability. While there are some questionable cases of conflict between states such as the conflict between Turkey and Greece over Cyprus in 1974, there has, so far, been no case that clearly disproves the Democratic Peace Theory. In fact, the Democratic Peace Theory is one of the few law-like rules in political science.

2.2   Qualitative and Quantitative Research

In the social sciences, we distinguish two large strands of research: quantitative and qualitative research. The major difference between these two research traditions is the number of observations. Research that involves few observations (e.g., one, two, or three individuals or countries) is generally referred to as qualitative. Such research requires an in-depth examination of the cases at hand. In contrast, work that includes hundreds, thousands, or even hundred thousand observations is generally called quantitative research. Quantitative research works with statistics or numbers that allow researchers to quantify the world. In the twenty-first century, statistics are nearly everywhere. In our daily lives, we encounter statistics in approval ratings of TV shows, the measurement of consumer preferences, weather forecasts, and betting odds, just to name a few examples. In social and political science research, statistics are the bread and butter of much scientific inquiry; statistics help us make sense of the world around us. For instance, in the political realm, we might gauge turnout rates as a measurement of the percentage of citizens that turned out during an election. In economics, some of the most important indicators about the state of the economy are monthly growth rates and consumer price indexes. In the field of education, the average grade of a student from a specific school gives an indication of the school's quality.

By using statistics, quantitative methods not only allow us to numerically describe phenomena, they also help us determine relationships between two or more variables. Examples of these relationships are multifold. For example, in the field of political science, statistics and quantitative methods have allowed us to detect that citizens who have a higher socioeconomic status (SES) are more likely to vote than individuals with a lower socioeconomic status (Milligan et al. 2004). In the field of economics, researchers have established with the help of quantitative analysis that low levels of corruption foster economic growth (Mo 2001). And in education research, there is near consensus in the quantitative research tradition that students from racially segregated areas and poor inner-city schools, on average, perform less strongly in college entry exams than students from rich, white neighborhoods (Rumberger and Palardy 2005).

Quantitative research is the primary tool to establish empirical relationships. However, it is less well-suited to explain the constituents or causal mechanism behind a statistical relationship. To highlight, quantitative research can illustrate that individuals with low education levels and below average income are less likely to vote compared to highly educated and rich citizens. Yet, it is less suitable to explain the reasons for their abstentions. Do they not feel represented? Are they fed up with how the system works? Do they not have the information and knowledge necessary to vote? Similarly, quantitative research robustly tells us that students in racially segregated areas tend to perform less strongly than students in predominantly white and wealthy neighborhoods. However, it does not tell us how the disadvantaged students feel about these inequalities and what they think can be done to reverse them. Are they enraged or fed up with the political regime and the politicians that represent it? Questions like these are better answered by qualitative research. The qualitative researcher wants to interpret the observational data (i.e., the fact that low SES individual has a higher likelihood to vote) and wants to grasp the opinions and attitudes of study subjects (i.e., how minority students feel in disadvantaged areas, how they think the system perpetuates these inequalities, and under what circumstances they are ready to protest). To gather this in-depth information, the qualitative researcher uses different techniques than the quantitative researchers. She needs research tools to tap into the opinions, perceptions, and feelings of study subjects. Tools appropriate for these inquiries are ethnographic methods including qualitative interviewing, participant observations, and the study of focus groups. These tools help us understand how individuals live, act, think, and feel in their natural setting and give meaning to quantitative findings.

In addition to allowing us to decipher meaning behind quantitative relationships, qualitative research techniques are an important tool in theory building. In fact, many research findings originate in qualitative research and are tested in a later stage in a quantitative large-N study. To take a classic in social sciences, Theda Skocpol offers in her seminal work *States and Social Revolutions: A comparative Analysis of Social Revolutions in Russia, France and China* (1979), an explanation for the occurrence of three important revolutions in the modern world, the French Revolution in 1789, the Chinese Revolution in 1911, and the Russian Revolution in 1917. Through historical analysis, Skocpol identifies three conditions for a revolution to happen: (1) a profound state crisis, (2) the emergence of a dominant class outside of the ruling elites, and (3) a state of severe economic and/or security crisis. Skocpol's book is an important exercise in theory building. She identifies three causal conditions, conditions that are quantifiable and that can be tested for other or all revolutions. By testing whether a profound state crisis, the emergence of a dominant class outside of the ruling elites, or a state of crisis explains other or all revolutions, quantitative researchers can establish the boundary conditions of Skocpol's theory.

It is also important to note that not all research is quantifiable. Some phenomena such as individual identities or ideologies are difficult to reduce to numbers: What are ethnic identities, religious identities, or regional identities? Often these critical concepts are not only difficult to identify but frequently also difficult to grasp empirically. For example, to understand what the regional francophone identity of

Quebecers is, we need to know the historical, social, and political context of the province and the fact that the province is surrounded by English speakers. To get a complete grasp of this regional identity, we, ideally, also have to retrace the recent development that more and more English is spoken in the major cities of Québec such as Montréal, particularly in the business world. These complexities are hard to reduce to numbers and need to be studied in-depth. For other events, there are just not enough observations to quantify them. For example, the Cold War is a unique event, an event that organized and shaped the world for 45 years in the twentieth century. Nearly, by definition this even is important and needs to be studied in-depth. Other events, like World War I and World War II, are for sure a subset of wars. However, these two wars have been so important for world history that, nearly by definition, they require in-depth study, as well. Both wars have shaped who we as individuals are (regardless where we live), what we think, how we act, and what we do. Hence, any bits of additional knowledge we acquire from these events not only help us understand the past but also help us move forward in the future.

Quantitative and qualitative methods are complimentary; students of the social sciences should master both techniques. However, it is hardly possible to do a thorough introduction into both. This book is about survey research, quantitative research tools, and statistics. It will teach you how to draft, conduct, and analyze a survey. However, before delving into the nuts and bolts of data analysis, we need to know what theories, hypotheses, concepts, and variables are. The next section will give you a short overview of these building blocks in social research.

2.3   Theories, Concepts, Variables, and Hypothesis

2.3.1   Theories

We have already learnt that social science research is cumulative. We build current knowledge on prior knowledge. Normally, we summarize our prior knowledge in theories, which are parsimonious or simplified explanations of how the world works. As such, a theory summarizes established knowledge in a specific field of study. Because the world around us is dynamic, a theory in the social sciences is never a deterministic statement. Rather it is open to revisions and amendments.[3] Theories can cover the micro-, meso-, and macro-levels. Below are three powerful social sciences theories.

Example of a Microlevel Theory: Relative Deprivation
Relative deprivation is a powerful individual-level theory to explain and predict citizens' participation in social movement activities. Relative deprivation starts with the premise that individuals do not protest, when they are happy with their lives.

---

[3]The idea behind parsimony is that scientists should rely on as few explanatory factors as possible while retaining a theory's generalizability.

Rather grievance theorists (e.g., Gurr 1970; Runciman 1966) see a discrepancy between value expectation and value capabilities as the root cause for protest activity. For example, according to Gurr (1970), individuals normally have no incentive to protest and voice their dissatisfaction if they are content with their daily lives. However, a deteriorating economic, social, or political situation can trigger frustrations, whether or real or perceived; the higher these frustrations are, the higher the likelihood that somebody will protest.

Example of a Meso-level Theory: The Iron Law of Oligarchy
The iron law of oligarchy is a political meso-level theory developed by German sociologist Robert Michels. His main argument is that over time all social groups, including trade unions and political parties, will develop hierarchical power structures or oligarchic tendencies. Stated differently, in any organization a "leadership class" consisting of paid administrators, spokespersons, societal elites, and organizers will prevail and centralize its power. And with power comes the possibility to control the laws and procedures of the organization and the information it communicates as well as the possibility to reward faithful members; all these tendencies are accelerated by apathetic masses, which will allow elites to hierarchize an organization faster (see Michels 1915).

Example of a Macro-level Theory: The Democratic Peace Theory
As discussed earlier in this chapter, a famous example of a macro-level theory is the so-called Democratic Peace Theory, which dates back to Kant's treatise on Perpetual Peace (1795). The theory states that democracies will not go to war with each other. It explicitly tackles the behavior of some type of state (i.e., democracies) and has only applicability at the macro-level.

Theory development is an iterative process. Because the world around us is dynamic (what is true today might no longer be true tomorrow), a theory must be perpetually tested and retested against reality. The more it is confirmed across time and space, the more it is robust. Theory building is a reiterative and lengthy process. Sometimes it takes years, if not decades to build and construct a theory. A famous example of how a theory can develop and refine is the simple rational choice theory of voting. In his 1957 famous book, *An Economic Theory of Democracy*, Anthony Downs tries to explain why some people vote, whereas others abstain from casting their ballots. Using a simple rational choice explanation, he concludes that voting is a "rational act" if the benefits of voting surpass the costs. To operationalize his theory, he defines the benefits of voting by the probability that an individual vote counts. The costs include the physical costs of actually leaving one's house and casting a ballot, as well as the ideational costs of gathering the necessary information to cast an educated ballot. While Downs finds his theory logical, he intuitively finds that there is something wrong with it. That is, the theory would predict that in the overall majority of cases, citizens should not vote, because in almost every case, the probability that an individual's vote will count is close to 0. Hence, the costs of voting surpass the benefits of voting for nearly every individual. However, Downs finds that in the majority people still vote, but does not have an immediate answer for this paradox of voting.

More than 10 years later, in a reformulation of Downs' theory, Riker and Ordeshook (1968) resolve Downs' paradox by adding an important component to Downs' model: the intangible benefits. According to the authors, the benefits of voting are not reduced to pure materialistic evaluations (i.e., the chance that a person's vote counts) but also to some nonmaterialistic benefits such as citizens' willingness to support democracy or the democratic system. Adding this additional component makes Down's theory more realistic and in tune with reality. On the negative side, adding nonmaterial benefits makes Down's theory less parsimonious. However, all researchers would probably agree that this sacrifice of parsimony is more than compensated for by the higher empirical applicability of the theory. Therefore, in this case the more complex theory is preferential to the more parsimonious theory. More generally, a theory should be as simple or parsimonious as possible and as complex as necessary.

2.3.2   Concepts

Theories are abstractions of objects, objects' properties, or behavioral phenomena. Any theory normally consists of at least two concepts, which define a theory's content and attributes. For example, the Democratic Peace Theory consists of the two concepts: democracy and war. Some concepts are concise (e.g., wealth, education, women's representation) and easier to measure, whereas other concepts are abstract (democracy, equal opportunity, human rights, social mobility, political culture) and more difficult to gauge. Whether abstract or precise, concepts provide a common language for political science. For sure, researchers might disagree about the precise (normative) definition of a concept. Nevertheless, they agree about its meaning. For example, if we talk about democracy, there is common understanding that we talk about a specific regime type that allows free and fair elections and some other freedoms. Nevertheless, there might be disagreement about the precise definition of the concept in question; in this case disagreement about democracy might revolve the following questions: do we only look at elections, do we include political rights, social rights, economic rights, or all of the above? To avoid any confusion, researchers must be precise when defining the meaning of a concept. In particular, this applies for contested concepts such as democracy. As already mentioned, for some scholars, the existence of parties, free and fair elections, and a reasonable participation by the population might be enough to classify a country as a democracy. For others, a country must have legally enforced guarantees for freedoms of speech, press, and religion and must guarantee social and economic rights. It can be either a normative or a practical question or both whether one or the other classification is more appropriate. It might also be a question of the specific research topic or research question, whether one or the other definition is more appropriate. Yet, whatever definition she chooses, a researcher must clearly identify and justify the choice of her definition, so that the reader of a published work can judge the appropriateness of the chosen definition.

It is also worth noting that the meaning of concepts can also change over time. Take again the example of democracy. Democracy 2000 years ago had a different meaning than democracy today. In the Greek city-states (e.g., Athens), democracy was a system of direct decision-making, in which all men above a certain income threshold convened on a regular basis to decide upon important matters such as international treaties, peace and war, as well as taxation. Women, servants, slaves, and poor citizens were not allowed to participate in these direct assemblies. Today, more than 2000 years after the Greek city-states, we commonly refer to democracy as a representative form of government, in which we elect members to parliament. In the elected assembly, these elected politicians should then represent the citizens that mandated them to govern. Despite the contention of how many political, civic, and social rights are necessary to consider a country a democracy, there is nevertheless agreement among academics and practitioners today that the Greek definition of democracy is outdated. In the twenty-first century, no serious academic would disagree that suffrage must be universal, each vote must count equally, and elections must be free and fair and must occur on a regular basis such as in a 4- or 5-year interval.

2.3.3 Variables

A variable refers to properties or attributes of a concept that can be measured in some way or another: in short, a variable is a measurable version of a concept. The process to transform a concept into a variable is called operationalization. To take an example, age is a variable, but the answer to the question how old you are is a variable. Some concepts in political or social science are rather easy to measure. For instance, on the individual level, somebody's education level can be measured by the overall years of schooling somebody has achieved or by the highest degree somebody has obtained. On the macro-level, women's representation in parliament can be easily measured by the percentage of seats in the elected assembly which are occupied by women. Other concepts, such as someone's political ideology on the individual level or democracy on the macro-level, are more difficult to measure. For example, operationalizations of political ideology range from the party one identifies with, to answers to survey questions about moral issues such as abortion or same-sex marriage, and to questions about whether somebody prefers more welfare state spending and higher taxes or less welfare state spending and lower taxes. For democracy, as already discussed, there is not only discussion of the precise definition of democracy but also on how to measure different regime types. For example, there is disagreement in the academic literature if we should adopt a dichotomous definition that distinguishes a democracy from a nondemocracy (Przeworski et al. 1996), a distinction in democracy, hybrid regime, or autocracy (Bollen 1990), or if we should use a graded measure, that is, democracy is not a question of kind, but of degree, and the gradation should capture sometimes partial processes of democratic institutions in many countries (Elkins 2000).

Table 2.1 Measuring Dahl's polyarchy

Components of democracy	Country 1	Country 2	Country 3
Elected officials have control over government decisions	x	–	x
Free, fair, and frequent elections	x	–	x
Universal suffrage	x	–	x
Right to run for office for all citizens	x	–	x
Freedom of expression	x	–	–
Alternative sources of information	x	–	–
Right to form and join autonomous political organizations	x	–	x
Polyarchy	Yes	No	No

When measuring a concept, it is important that a concept has high content validity; there should be a high degree of convergence between the measure and the concept it is thought to represent. In other words, a high content validity is achieved if a measure represents all facets of a given concept. To highlight how this convergence can be achieved, I use one famous definition of democracy, Dahl's polyarchy. Polyarchy, according to Dahl, is a form of representative democracy characterized by a particular set of political institutions. These include elected officials, free and fair elections, inclusive suffrage, the right to run for office, freedom of expression, alternative information, and associational autonomy (see Dahl 1973). To achieve high content validity, any measurement of polyarchy must include the seven dimensions of democracy; that is, any of these seven dimensions must be explicitly measured. Sometimes a conceptual definition predisposes researchers to use one operationalization of a concept over another one. In Dahl's classification, the respect of the seven features is a minimum standard for democracy; that is why his concept of polyarchy is best operationalized dichotomously. That is, a country is a polyarchy if it respects all of the seven features and is not if it doesn't (i.e., it is enough to not qualify as a democracy if one of the features is not respected). Table 2.1 graphically displays this logic. Only country 1 respects all features of a polyarchy and can be classified as such. Countries 2 and 3 violate some or all of these minimum conditions of polyarchy and hence must be coded as nondemocracies.

Achieving high content validity is not always easy. Some concepts are difficult to measure. Take the concept of political corruption. Political corruption, or the private (mis)use of public funds for illegitimate private gains, happens behind closed doors without the supervision of the public. Nearly by definition this entails that nearly all proxy variables to measure corruption are imperfect. There are at least three ways to measure corruption:

1. Large international efforts compiled by international organizations such as the World Bank or Transparency International try to track corruption in the public sector around the globe. For example, the Corruption Perceptions Index (CPI)

focuses on corruption in the public sector. It uses expert surveys with country experts inside and outside the country under scrutiny on, among others, bribery of public officials, kickbacks in public procurement, embezzlement of public funds, and the strength and effectiveness of public sector anti-corruption efforts. It then creates a combined measure from these surveys.

2. National agencies in several (Western) countries track data on the number of federal, state, and local government officials prosecuted and convicted for corruption crimes.

3. International public opinion surveys (e.g., the World Value Survey) ask citizens about their own experience with corruption (e.g., if they have paid or received a bribe to or for any public service within the past 12 months).

Any of these three measurements is potentially problematic. First, perception indexes based on interviews/surveys with country experts can be deceiving, as there is no hard evidence to back up claims of high or low corruption, even if these assessments come from so-called experts. However, the hard evidence can be deceiving as well. Are many corruption charges and indictments a sign of high or low corruption? They might be a sign of high corruption, as it shows corruption is widespread; a certain percentage of the officials in the public sector engage in the exchange of public goods for private promotion. Yet, many cases treated in court might also be a sign of low corruption. It might show that the system works, as it cracks down on corrupted officials. For the third measure, citizens' personal experience with corruption is suboptimal, as well. Given that corruption is a shameful act, survey participants might not admit that they have participated in fraudulent activities. They might also fear repercussions by the public if they admit being part of a corrupt network. Finally, it might not be rational to admit corruption, particularly if you are one of the beneficiaries of it.

In particular, for difficult to measure concepts such as corruption, it might be advisable to cross-validate any imperfect proxy with another measure. In other words, different measures must resemble each other if they tap into the same concept. If this is the case, we speak of high construct validity, and it is possibly safe to use one proxy or even better create a conjoint index of the proxy variables in question. If this is not the case, then there is a problem with one or several measurements, something the researcher should assess in detail. One way to measure whether two measurements of the same variable are strongly related to each other is through correlation analysis (see Chap. 8).

Sometimes it is not only difficult to achieve high operational validity of difficult concepts such as corruption but sometimes also for seemingly simple concepts such as voting or casting a ballot for a radical right-wing party. In answering a survey, individuals might pretend they have voted or cast a ballot for a mainstream party to pretend that they abide by the societal norms. Yet it is very difficult to detect the type of individuals, who either deliberately or undeliberately answer a survey question incorrectly (for a broader discussion of biases in survey research, see Sect. 5.2).

2.3.3.1 Types of Variables

In empirical research we distinguish two main types of variables: dependent variable and independent variable.

Dependent Variable The dependent variable is the variable the researcher is trying to explain. It is the primary variable of interest and depends on other variables (so-called independent variables). In quantitative studies, the dependent variable has the notation y.

Independent Variable Independent variables are hypothesized to explain variation in the dependent variable. Because they are thought to explain variation or changes in the dependent variable, independent variables are sometimes also called explanatory variables (as they should explain the dependent variable). In quantitative studies, the independent variable has the notation x.

I use another famous theory, modernization theory, to explain the difference between independent and dependent variable. In essence, modernization theory states that countries with a higher degree of development are more likely to be democratic (Lipset 1959). In this example, the dependent variable is regime type (however measured). The independent variable is a country's level of development, which could, for instance, be measured by a country's GDP per capita.

In the academic literature, independent variables that are not the focus of the study, but which might also have an influence on the dependent variable, are sometimes referred to as control variables. To take an example from the turnout literature, a researcher might be interested in the relationship between electoral competitiveness and voter turnout. Electoral competitiveness is the independent variable, and turnout is the dependent variable. However, turnout rates in countries or electoral districts are not only dependent on the competiveness of the election (which is often operationalized by the difference in votes between the winner and the runner-up) but also by a host of other factors including compulsory voting, the electoral system type, corruption, or income inequalities, to name a few factors. These other independent variables must also be accounted for and included in the study. In fact, researchers can only test the "real impact" of competitiveness on turnout, if they also take these other factors into consideration.

2.3.4   Hypotheses

A hypothesis is a tentative, provisional, or unconfirmed statement derived from theory that can (in principle) be either verified or falsified. It explicitly states the expected relationship between an independent and dependent variable. Hypotheses must be empirically testable statements that can cover any level of analysis. In fact, a good hypothesis should specify the types or level of political actor to which the hypothesis will test (see also Table 2.2).

Table 2.2 Examples of good and bad hypotheses

Wrong	Right
Democracy is the best form of government	The more democratic a country is, the better its government performance will be
The cause of civil war is economic upheaval	The more there is economic upheaval, the more likely a country will experience civil war
Raising the US minimum wage will affect job growth	Raising the minimum wage will create more jobs (positive relationship) Raising the minimum wage will cut jobs (negative relationship)

Macro-level An example of a macro-level hypothesis derived from modernization theory would be: The more highly developed a country, the more likely it is a democracy.

Meso-level An example of a meso-level hypothesis derived from the iron law of oligarchy would be: The longer a political or social organization is in existence, the more hierarchical are its power structures.

Microlevel An example of a microlevel hypothesis derived from the resource theory of voting would be: The higher somebody's level of education, the more likely they are to vote.

Scientific hypotheses are always stated in the following form:

The more [independent variable], the more [dependent variable] **or** the more [independent variable], the less [dependent variable].

When researchers formulate hypotheses, they make three explicit statements:

1. *X* and *Y* covary. This implies that there is variation in the independent and dependent variable and that at least some of the variation in the dependent variable is explained by variation in the independent variable.
2. Change in *X* precedes change in *Y*. By definition a change in independent variable can only trigger a change in the dependent variable if this change happens before the change in the dependent variable.
3. The effect of the independent variable on the dependent variable is not coincidental or spurious (which means explained by other factors) but direct.

To provide an example, the resource theory of voting states that individuals with higher socioeconomic status (SES) are more likely to vote. From this theory, I can derive the microlevel hypothesis that the more educated a citizen is, the higher the chance that she will cast a ballot. To be able to test this hypothesis, I operationalize SES by a person's years of full-time schooling and voting by a survey question asking whether somebody voted or not in the last national election. By formulating this hypothesis, I make the implicit assumption that there is variation in the overall years of schooling and variation in voting. I also explicitly state that the causal explanatory chain goes from education to voting (i.e., that education precedes voting). Finally, I expect that changes in somebody's education trigger changes in somebody's likelihood to vote (i.e., I expect the relationship to not be spurious). While for the resource hypothesis, there is probably consensus that the causal chain goes from more education to a higher likelihood to vote, and not the other way around, the same does not apply to all empirical relationships. Rather, in political science we do not always have a one-directional relationship. For example, regarding the modernization hypothesis, there is some debate in the scholarly community surrounding whether it is development that triggers the installation of democracy or if it is democracy that triggers robust economic development more than any other regime type. There are statistical methods to treat cases of reversed causation such as structural equation modelling. Because of the advanced nature of these techniques, I will not cover these techniques in this book. Nevertheless, what is important to take away from this discussion is that students of political science and the social sciences, more generally, must think carefully about the direction of cause and effect before they formulate a hypothesis.

It is also important that students know the difference between an alternative hypothesis and a null hypothesis. The alternative hypothesis, sometimes also called research hypothesis, is the hypothesis you are going to test. The null hypothesis is the rival hypothesis—it assumes that there is no association between the independent and dependent variables. To give an example derived from the iron law of oligarchy, a researcher wanting to test this theory could postulate the hypothesis that "the longer a political organization is in existence, the more hierarchical it will get." In social science jargon, this hypothesis is called the alternative hypothesis. The corresponding null-hypothesis would be that length of existence of a political organization and its hierarchical structure are unrelated.

2.4   The Quantitative Research Process

The quantitative research process is deductive (see Fig. 2.1). It is theory driven; it starts and ends with theory. Before the start of any research project, students of political science must know the relevant literatures. They must know the dominant theories and explanations of the phenomenon they want to study and identify controversies and holes or gaps in knowledge. The existing theory will then guide them to formulate some hypotheses that will ideally try to resolve some of the controversies or fill one or several gaps in knowledge. Quantitative research might also test existing theories with new quantitative data, establish the boundaries or limitations of a theory, or establish the conditions under which a theory applies. Whatever its purpose, good research starts with a theoretically derived research question and hypothesis. Ideally, the research question should address a politically relevant and important topic and make a potential theoretical contribution to the literature (it should potentially add to, alter, change, or refute the existing theory). The hypothesis should clearly identify the independent and dependent variable. It should be a plausible statement of how the researcher thinks that the independent

Fig. 2.1 Display of the quantitative research process

variable behaves toward the dependent variable. In addition, the researcher must also identify potential control variables. In the next step, the researcher has to think about how to measure independent, dependent, and control variables. When operationalizing her variables, she must ensure that there is high content validity between the numerical representation and the conceptional definition of any given concept. After having decided how to measure the variables, the researcher has to think about sampling. In other words, which empirical referents will she use to test her hypothesis? Measurement and sampling are often done concurrently, because the empirical referents, which the researchers study, might predispose her to use one operationalization of an indicator over another. Sometimes, also practical consider-ations such as the existence of empirical data determine the measurement of variables and the number and type of observations studied. Once the researcher has her data, she can then conduct the appropriate statistical tests to evaluate research question and hypothesis. The results of her study will then ideally have an influence on theory.

Let us explain Fig. 2.1 with a concrete example. We assume that a researcher is interested in individuals' participation in demonstrations. Reading the literature, she finds two dominant theories. On the one hand, the resource theory of political action states that the more resources individuals have in the form of civic skills, network connections, time, and money, the more likely they are to engage in collective political activities including partaking in demonstrations. On the other hand, the relative deprivation approach states that individuals must be frustrated with their economic, social, and political situation. The more they see a gap between value expectations and value capabilities, the more likely they are going to protest. Implicit in the second argument is that individuals in the bottom echelon of society such as the unemployed, those who struggle economically, or those who are deprived of equal chances in society such as minorities are more likely to demonstrate. Having identified this controversy, the researcher asks himself which, if either, of the two competing theories is more correct. Because the researcher does not know, a priori, which of the two theories is more likely to apply, she formulates two competing hypotheses:

Hypothesis 1: The higher somebody's SES, the higher somebody's likelihood to partake in a demonstration.

Hypothesis 2: The higher somebody's dissatisfaction with her daily life, the higher the likelihood that this person will demonstrate.

Having formulated her hypotheses, the researcher has to identify other potentially relevant variables that could explain one's decision to partake in a demonstration. From the academic literature on protest, she identifies gender, age, political socialization, and place of residency as other potentially relevant variables which she also has to include/control for in her study. Once the hypotheses are formulated and control variables identified, the researcher then has to determine the measurement of the main variables of interest and for the control variables before finding an appropriate study sample. To measure the first independent variable, a person's SES, the researcher decides to employ two very well-known proxy variables, education and income. For the second, independent variable, she thinks that the survey question "how satisfied are you with your daily life" captures individuals' levels of frustrations pretty well. The dependent variable, partaking in a demonstration, could be measured by a survey question asking whether somebody has demonstrated within the past year. Because the researcher finds that the European Social Survey (ESS) asks all these questions using a representative sample of individuals in about 20 European countries, she uses this sample as the study object or data source. She then engages in appropriate statistical techniques to gauge the influence of her two main variables of interest on the dependent variable. As a preliminary test, she must also test her assumption that people with poor SES are more likely to be frustrated and dissatisfied with their lives. Let us assume she finds through appropriate statistical analysis that it is in fact less educated and lower-income individuals who are more likely to be dissatisfied and who demonstrate more. Finding this, the researcher would resolve some of the controversy around the two contradictory hypotheses for partaking in demonstrations, at least when it comes to the European countries under consideration.

References

Beetham, D. (1999). *Democracy and human rights*. Cambridge: Polity.

Bogaards, M. (2007). Measuring democracy through election outcomes: A critique with African data. *Comparative Political Studies, 40*(10), 1211–1237.

Bollen, K. A. (1990). Political democracy: Conceptual and measurement traps. *Studies in Comparative International Development (SCID), 25*(1), 7–24.

Chandler, D. (2010). The uncritical critique of 'liberal peace'. *Review of International Studies, 36*(1), 137–155.

Daase, C. (2006). Democratic peace—Democratic war: Three reasons why democracies are war-prone. In *Democratic wars* (pp. 74–89). London: Palgrave Macmillan.

Dahl, R. A. (1973). *Polyarchy: Participation and opposition*. Yale: Yale University Press.

De Mesquita, B. B., Morrow, J. D., Siverson, R. M., & Smith, A. (1999). An institutional explanation of the democratic peace. *American Political Science Review, 93*(4), 791–807.

Downs, A. (1957). An economic theory of political action in a democracy. *Journal of Political Economy, 65*(2), 135–150.

Elkins, Z. (2000). Gradations of democracy? Empirical tests of alternative conceptualizations. *American Journal of Political Science, 44*(2), 293–300.

Gleditsch, N. E. (2002). Armed conflict 1946–2001: A new dataset. *Journal of Peace Research, 39*(5), 615–637.

Gurr, T. R. (1970). *Why men rebel*. Princeton: Princeton University Press.

Kant, I. (1795) [2011]. *Zum ewigen Frieden*. (3rd ed.). Berlin: Akademie Verlag.

Lipset, S. L. (1959). Some social requisites of democracy: Economic development and political legitimacy. *American Political Science Review, 53*(1), 69–105.

Mansfield, E. D., & Snyder, J. (2007). *Electing to fight: Why emerging democracies go to war*. Boston: MIT Press.

Marshall, M. G., Jaggers, K., & Gurr, T. R. (2011). *Polity IV project: Dataset users' manual*. Arlington: Polity IV Project.

Michels, R. (1915). *Political parties: A sociological study of the oligarchical tendencies of modern democracy*. New York: The Free Press.

Milligan, K., Moretti, E., & Oreopoulos, P. (2004). Does education improve citizenship? Evidence from the United States and the United Kingdom. *Journal of Public Economics, 88*(9), 1667–1695.

Mo, P. H. (2001). Corruption and economic growth. *Journal of Comparative Economics, 29*(1), 66–79.

Przeworski, A., Alvarez, M., Cheibub, J. A., & Linongi, F. (1996). What makes democracies endure? *Journal of Democracy, 7*(1), 39–55.

Riker, W. H., & Ordeshook, P. C. (1968). A theory of the calculus of voting. *American Political Science Review, 62*(1), 25–42.

Rumberger, R. W., & Palardy, G. J. (2005). Does segregation still matter? The impact of student composition on academic achievement in high school. *Teachers College Record, 107*(9), 1999.

Runciman, W. G. (1966). *Relative deprivation and social injustice. A study of attitudes to social inequality in twentieth century England*. London: Routledge and Keagan Paul.

Russett, B. (1994). *Grasping the democratic peace: Principles for a post-cold war world*. Princeton: Princeton University Press.

Skocpol, T. (1979). *States and social revolutions: A comparative analysis of France, Russia and China. Cambridge*: Cambridge University Press.

Walsh, A., & Ollenburger, J. C. (2001). *Essential statistics for the social and behavioral sciences: A conceptual approach*. Prentice Hall: Pearson Education.

Further Reading

Research Design

Creswell, J. W., & Creswell, J. D. (2017). *Research design: Qualitative, quantitative, and mixed methods approaches*. Thousand Oaks, CA: Sage. Nice introduction into the two main research traditions qualitative and quantitative research. The book also covers mixed methods' approaches (approaches that combine qualitative and quantitative methods).

McNabb, D. E. (2015). *Research methods for political science: Quantitative and qualitative methods*. London: Routledge (Chap. 7). Nice introduction into the nuts and bolts of quantitative methods. Introduces basic concepts such as reliability and validity, as well as discusses different types of statistics (i.e. inferential statistics).

Shively, W. P. (2016). *The craft of political research*. New York: Routledge. Precise and holistic introduction into the quantitative research process.

Theories and Hypotheses

Brians, C. L., Willnat, L., Manheim, J., & Rich, R. (2016). *Empirical political analysis*. London: Routledge (Chaps. 2, 4, 5). Comprehensive introduction into theories, hypothesis testing and operationalization of variables.

Qualitative Research

Elster, J. (1989). *Nuts and bolts for the social sciences*. Cambridge: Cambridge University Press. A nice introduction into causal explanations and causal mechanisms. The book explains what causal mechanisms are and what research steps the researcher can conduct to detect them.

Gerring, J. (2004). What is a case study and what is it good for?. American political science review, 98(2), 341–354. A nice introduction on what a case study is, what is good for in political science, and what different types of case studies exist.

Lijphart, A. (1971). Comparative politics and the comparative method. *American Political Science Review*, 65(3), 682–693. Seminal work on the comparative case study. Explains what a comparative case study is, how it relates to the field of comparative politics, and how to conduct a comparative case study.

A Short Introduction to Survey Research

3

Abstract

This chapter offers a brief introduction into survey research. In the first part of the chapter, students learn about the importance of survey research in the social and behavioral sciences, substantive research areas where survey research is frequently used, and important cross-national survey such as the World Values Survey and the European Social Survey. In the second, I introduce different types of surveys.

3.1 What Is Survey Research?

Survey research has become a major, if not the main, technique to gather information about individuals of all sorts. To name a few examples:

- **Costumer surveys** ask individuals about their purchasing habits or their satisfaction with a product or service. Such surveys can gain and reveal consumer habits and inform marketing strategies by companies.
- **Attitudinal surveys** poll participants on social, economic, or cultural attitudes. These surveys are important for researchers and policy makers as they allow us to detect cultural values, political attitudes, and social preferences.
- **Election surveys** ask citizens about their voting habits. As such they can, for example, influence campaign strategies by parties.

Regardless of its type, survey research involves the systematic collection of information from individuals using standardized procedures. When conducting survey research, the researcher normally uses a (random or representative) sample from the population she wants to study and asks the survey subjects one or several questions about attitudes, perceptions, or behaviors. In the ideal case, she wants to produce a set of data on a given phenomenon that captures the studied concept, as

© Springer International Publishing AG 2019

D. Stockemer, *Quantitative Methods for the Social Sciences*,

https://doi.org/10.1007/978-3-319-99118-4_3

well as relevant independent variables. She also wants to have a sample that describes the population she wants to study fairly well (Fowler 2009: 1). To provide a concrete example, if a researcher wants to gather information on the popularity of the German chancellor, she has to collect a sufficiently large sample that is representative of the German population (see Chap. 4 for a discussion of representativeness). She might ask individuals to rate the popularity of the German chancellor on a 0–100 scale. She might also ask respondents about their gender, age, income, education, and place of residency to determine what types of individuals like the head of the German government more and what groups like her less. If these data are collected on a regular basis, it also allows researchers to gain relevant information about trends in societies. For example, so-called trend studies allow researchers to track the popularity of the chancellor over time and possibly to associate increases and decreases in her popularity with political events such as the German reunification in 1990 or the refugee crisis in Germany in 2015.

3.2 A Short History of Survey Research

The origins of survey research go back thousands of years. These origins are linked to the understanding that every society with some sort of bureaucracy, in order to function properly, needs some information about its citizens. For example, in order to set taxation levels and plan infrastructure, bureaucracies need to know basic information about their citizens such as how many citizens live in a geographical unit, how much money they earn, and how many acres of land they own. Hints on first data collection efforts date back to the great civilizations of antiquity, such as China, Egypt, Persia, Greece, or the Roman Empire. A famous example of early data collection is the census mentioned in the bible during the time of Jesus' birth:

> In those days a decree went out from Emperor Augustus that all the world should be registered. This was the first registration and was taken while Quirinius was governor of Syria. All went to their own towns to be registered. Joseph also went from the town of Nazareth in Galilee to Judea, to the city of David called Bethlehem, because he was descended from the house and family of David. He went to be registered with Mary, to whom he was engaged and who was expecting a child. (Luke 2:1–5)

While it is historically unclear whether the census by Emperor Augustus was actually held at the time of Jesus' birth, the citation from the bible nevertheless shows that as early as in the ancient times, governments tried to retrieve information about their citizens. To do so, families had to register in the birth place of the head of the family and answer some questions which already resembled our census questions today.

In the middle ages, data collection efforts and surveys became more sophisticated. England took a leading role in this process. The first Norman king, William the Conqueror, was a leading figure in this quest. After his conquest of England in 1066, he strived to gather knowledge on the property conditions, as well as the yearly income of the barons and cities in the seized territories. For example, he wanted to know how many acres of land the barons owned so that he could determine appropriate taxes. In the following centuries, the governing processes became increasingly centralized. To run their country efficiently and to defend the country against external threats, the absolutist English rulers depended on extensive data on labor, military capabilities, and trade (Hooper 2006). While some of these data were "hard data" collected directly from official books (e.g., the manpower of the army), other data, for example, on military capabilities, trade returns, or the development of the population, were, at least in part, retrieved through survey questions or interviews. Regardless of its nature, the importance of data collection rose, in particularly, in the economic and military realms. London was the first city, where statistics were systematically applied to some collected data. In the seventeenth century, economists including John Graunt, William Petty, and Edmund Halley tried to estimate population developments on the basis of necrologies and birth records. These studies are considered to be the precursors of modern quantitative analysis with the focus on causal explanations (Petty and Graunt 1899).

Two additional societal developments rendered the necessity for good data the more urgent. First, the adaption of a data-based capitalist economic system in the eighteenth and nineteenth century accelerated data collection efforts in England and later elsewhere in Europe. The rationalization of administrative planning processes in many European countries further increased the need to gain valid data, not only about the citizens but also about the administrative processes. Again, some of these data could only be collected by asking others. The next boost then occurred in the early nineteenth century. The Industrial Revolution combined with urbanization had created high levels of poverty for many residents in large British cities such as Manchester or Birmingham. To get some "valid picture" of the diffusion of poverty, journalists collected data by participating in poor people's lives, asking them questions about their living standard and publishing their experiences. This development resulted in the establishment of "statistical societies" in most large English cities (Wilcox 1934). Although the government shut down most of these statistical societies, it was pressed to extend its own data gathering by introducing routine data collections on births, deaths, and crime. Another element of these developments was the implementation of enquete commissions whose work looked at these abominable living conditions in some major English cities and whose conclusions were partly based on quantitative data gathered by asking people questions about their lives. Similar developments happened elsewhere, as well. A prominent example is the empirical research of medical doctors in Germany in the nineteenth century, who primarily examined the living and working conditions of laborers and the health-care system (Schnell et al. 2011: 13–20).

Despite these efforts, it was not until the early twentieth century until political opinion polling in the way we conduct it today was born. Opinion polling in its contemporary form has its roots in the United States of America (USA). It started in the early twentieth century, when journalists attempted to forecast the outcomes of presidential elections. Initially, the journalists just took the assessment of some citizens before newspapers came up with more systematic approaches to predict the election results. *The Literary Digest* was the first newspaper to distribute a large number of postal surveys among voters in 1916 (Converse 2011). The poll also correctly predicted the winner of the 1916 Presidential Elections, Woodrow Wilson. This survey was the first mass survey in the United States and the first systematic opinion poll in the country's history (Burnham et al. 2008: 99 f.). At about the same time, the British philanthropists Charles Booth and Seebohm Rowntree chose interview approaches to explain the causes of poverty. What distinguishes their works from former studies is the close link between social research and political application. To a get valid picture of poverty in the English city of York, Rowntree attempted to interview all working-class people living in York. Of course, this was a long and tiring procedure that took several years. The Rowntree example rendered it very clear to researchers, journalists, and data collection organizations that collecting data on the population researchers want to study is very cumbersome and difficult to do. Consequently, this method of data collection has become very exceptional (Burnham et al. 2008: 100 f.; Schnell et al. 2011: 21–23). Due to the immense costs associated with complete enumerations, only governments have the means to carry them out today (e.g., through the census). Researchers must rely mainly on samples, which they use to draw inferences on population statistics. Building on the work of *The Literary Digest*, in the USA and various efforts on the continent, the twentieth century has seen a refinement of survey and sampling techniques and their broad application to many different scenarios, be they economic, social, or political. Today surveys are ubiquitous. There is probably not one adult individual in the Western world who has not been asked at least once in her lifetime to participate in a survey.

3.3 The Importance of Survey Research in the Social Sciences and Beyond

Survey research is one of the pillars in social science research in the twenty-first century. Surveys are used to measure almost everything from voting behavior to public opinion and to sexual preferences (De Leeuw et al. 2008: 1). They are of interest to a wide range of constituents including citizens, parties, civil society organizations, and governments. Individuals might be interested in situating their beliefs and behavior in relation to those of their peers and societies. Parties might want to know which party is ahead in the public preference at any given point in time and what the policy preferences of citizens are. Civil society organizations might use surveys to give credence to their lobbying points. Governments at various levels (i.e., the federal, regional, or local) may use surveys to find out how the public judges their performance or how popular specific policy proposals are among the general public. In short, surveys are ubiquitous in social and political life (for a good description of the importance of survey research, see Archer and Berdahl 2011).

Opinion polls help us to situate ourselves with regard to others in different social settings. On the one hand, survey research allows us to compare our social norms and ideals in Germany, Western Europe, or the Americas to those in Japan, China, or Southeast Asia. For example, analyzing data from a general cross-national social survey provides us with an opportunity to compare attitudes and social behaviors across countries; for instance, we can compare whether we eat more fast food, watch more television, have more pets, or believe more in extensive social welfare than citizens in Australia or Asia. Yet, not only does survey research allow us to detect between country variation in opinions, beliefs, and behaviors but also within a country, if the sample is large enough. In Germany, for example, large-scale surveys can detect if individuals in the East have stronger anti-immigrant attitudes than individuals in the West. In the United States, opinion polls can identify whether the approval rating of President Trump is higher in Texas than in Connecticut. Finally, opinion polls can serve to detect differences in opinion between different cohorts of the population. For example, we can compare how much trust young people (i.e., individuals in the age cohort 18–25) have into the military compared to senior citizens (i.e., individuals aged 60 and older) both for one country and for several countries.

Survey research has also shaped the social- and political sciences. To illustrate, I will just introduce two classic works in political science, whose findings and conclusions are primarily based on survey research. First, one of the most outstanding political treatises based on survey research is *The Civic Culture* by Gabriel Almond and Sidney Verba (1963). In their study, the authors use surveys on political orientations about the political systems (e.g., opinions, attitudes, and values) to detect that cultural norms must be congruent with the political system to ensure the stability of the system in question. Another classic using survey research is Robert Putnam's *Bowling Alone; The collapse and revival of American community* (2001). Mainly through survey research, Putnam finds that social engagement had weakened in the United States during the late twentieth century. He links the drop in all types of social and political activities to a decrease in membership in all kinds of organizations (e.g., social, political, or community organizations), declining contract among individuals (e.g., among neighbors, friends, and family), less volunteering, and less religious involvement. It should also be noted that survey research is not only a stand-alone tool to answer many relevant research questions, it can also be combined with other types of research such as qualitative case studies or the analysis of hard macro-level data. In a prime example of mixed methods, Wood (2003), aiming to understand the peasant's rationales in El Salvador to join revolutionary movements in the country's civil war, uses first ethnographic interviews of some peasants in a specific region to tap into these motivations. In a later stage, she employs large national household surveys to confirm the conclusions derived from the interviews.

3.4   Overview of Some of the Most Widely Used Surveys in the Social Sciences

Governments, governmental and non-governmental organizations, and social research centers spend millions of dollars per year to conduct cross-national surveys. These surveys (e.g., the World Values Survey or the European Social Survey) use representative or random samples of individuals in many countries to detect trends in individuals' social and political opinions, as well as their social and political behavior. We can distinguish different types of surveys. First, behavioral surveys measure individuals' political-related, health-related, or job-related behavior. Probably most prominent in the field of political science, election surveys gauge individuals' conventional and unconventional political activities in a regional, national, or international context (e.g., whether somebody participates in elections, engages in protest activity, or contacts a political official). Other behavioral surveys might capture health risk behaviors, employee habits, or drug use, just to name few. Second, opinion surveys try to capture opinions and beliefs in a society; these questionnaires aim at gauging individual opinions on a variety of topics ranging from consumer behavior to public preferences, to political ideologies, and to preferred free time activities and preferred vacation spots.

Below, I present three of the most widely used surveys in political science and possibly the social sciences more generally: the Comparative Study of Electoral Systems (CSES), the World Values Survey (WVS), and the European Social Survey (ESS). Hundreds, if not thousands, of articles have emanated from these surveys. In these large-scale research projects, the researcher's duties include the composition of the questionnaire and the selection and training of the interviewers. The latter functions as the link between researcher and respondent. They run the interviews and should record the responses precisely and thoroughly (Loosveldt 2008: 201).

3.4.1   The Comparative Study of Electoral Systems (CSES)

The Comparative Study of Electoral Systems (CSES) is a collaborative program of cross-national research among election studies conducted in over 50 states. The CSES is composed of three tightly linked parts: first, a common module of public opinion survey questions is included in each participant country's post-election study. These "microlevel" data include vote choice, candidate and party evaluations, current and retrospective economic evaluations, evaluations of the electoral system itself, and standardized sociodemographic measures. Second, district-level data are reported for each respondent, including electoral returns, turnout, and the number of candidates. Finally, system- or "macro-level" data report aggregate electoral returns, electoral rules and formulas, and regime characteristics. This design allows researchers to conduct cross-level and cross-national analyses, addressing the effects of electoral institutions on citizens' attitudes and behavior, the presence and nature of social and political cleavages, and the evaluation of democratic institutions across different political regimes.

The CSES is unique among comparative post-electoral studies because of the extent of cross-national collaboration at all stages of the project: the research agenda, the survey instrument, and the study design are developed by the CSES Planning Committee, whose members include leading scholars of electoral politics from around the world. This design is then implemented in each country by that country's foremost social scientists, as part of their national post-election studies. Frequently, the developers of the survey decide upon a theme for any election cycle. For example, the initial round of collaboration focused on three general themes: the impact of electoral institutions on citizens' political cognition and behavior (parliamentary versus presidential systems of government, the electoral rules that govern the casting and counting of ballots and political parties), the nature of political and social cleavages and alignments, and the evaluation of democratic institutions and processes. The key theoretical question to be addressed by the second module is the contrast between the view that elections are a mechanism to hold government accountable and the view that they are a means to ensure that citizens' views and interests are properly represented in the democratic process. It is the module's aim to explore how far this contrast and its embodiment in institutional structures influences vote choice and satisfaction with democracy.

The CSES can be accessed at http://www.isr.umich.edu/cps/project_cses.html.

3.4.2   The World Values Survey (WVS)

The World Values Survey is a global research project that explores peoples' values and beliefs, how they change over time, and what social and political impact they have. It emerged in 1981 and was mainly coined by the scientists Ronald Inglehart, Jan Kerkhofs, and Ruud de Moor. The survey's focus was initially on European countries, although since the late 1990s, however, non-European countries have received more attention. Today, more than 80 independent countries representing 85% of the world's population are included in the survey (Hurtienne and Kaufmann 2015: 9 f.). The survey is carried out by a worldwide network of social scientists who, since 1981, have conducted representative national surveys in multiple waves in over 80 countries. The WVS measures, monitors, and analyzes a host of issues including support for democracy; tolerance of foreigners and ethnic minorities; support for gender equality; the role of religion and changing levels of religiosity; the impact of globalization; attitudes toward the environment, work, family, politics, national identity, culture, diversity, and insecurity; and subjective well-being on the basis of face-to-face interviews. The questionnaires are distributed among 1100–3500 interviewees per country. The findings are valuable for policy makers seeking to build civil society and democratic institutions in developing countries. The work is also frequently used by governments around the world, scholars, students, journalists, and international organizations and institutions such as the World Bank and the United Nations (UNDP and UN-Habitat). Thanks to the increasing number of participating countries and the growing time period that the WVS covers, the WVS satisfies (some of) the demand for cross-sectional attitudinal data. The application of WVS data in hundreds of publications and in more than 20 languages stresses the crucial role that the WVS plays in scientific research today (Hurtienne and Kaufmann 2015: 9 f.).

The World Values Survey can be accessed at http://www.worldvaluessurvey.org/.

3.4.3   The European Social Survey (ESS)

The European Social Survey (ESS) is an academically driven cross-national survey
that has been conducted every 2 years across Europe since 2001. It is directed by
Rory Fitzgerald (City University London). The survey measures the attitudes,
beliefs, and behavioral patterns of diverse populations in more than 30 European
nations. As the largest data collection effort in and on Europe, the ESS has five aims:

1. To chart stability and change in social structure, conditions, and attitudes in
   Europe and to interpret how Europe's social, political, and moral fabric is
   changing.
2. To achieve and spread higher standards of rigor in cross-national research in the
   social sciences, including, for example, questionnaire design and pre-testing,
   sampling, data collection, reduction of bias, and the reliability of questions.
3. To introduce soundly based indicators of national progress, based on citizens'
   perceptions and judgements of key aspects of their societies.
4. To undertake and facilitate the training of European social researchers in comparative quantitative measurement and analysis.
5. To improve the visibility and outreach of data on social change among academics,
   policy makers, and the wider public.

The findings of the ESS are based on face-to-face interviews, and the questionnaire is comprised of three sections, a core module, two rotating modules, and a
supplementary questionnaire. The core module comprises questions on the media
and social trust, politics, the subjective well-being of individuals, gender and
household dynamics, sociodemographics, and social values. As such, the core
module should capture topics that are of enduring interest for researchers as well
as provide the most comprehensive set of socio-structural variables in a cross-
national survey worldwide. The two rotating modules capture "hot" social science
topics; for example, rotating modules in 2002 and 2014 focused on immigration,
while the 2016 wave captures European citizens' attitudes about welfare and
opinions toward climate change. The purpose of the supplementary questionnaire
at the end of the survey is to elaborate in more detail on human values and to test the
reliability and validity of the items in the principal questionnaire on the basis of some
advanced statistical techniques (ESS 2017).
    The European Social Survey can be accessed at http://www.
europeansocialsurvey.org/.

3.5   Different Types of Surveys

For political science students, it is important to realize that one survey design does
not necessarily resemble another survey design. Rather, in survey research, we
generally distinguish between two types of surveys: cross-sectional surveys and
longitudinal surveys (see Frees 2004: 2).

3.5.1 Cross-sectional Survey

A cross-sectional survey is a survey that is used to gather information about individuals at a single point in time. The survey is conducted once and not repeated. An example of a cross-sectional survey would be a poll that asks respondents in the United States how much they donated toward the reconstruction efforts after Hurricane Katrina hit the Southern States of the United States. Surveys, such as the one capturing donation patterns in the aftermath of Hurricane Katrina, are particularly interesting to seize attitudes and behaviors related to one event that probably will not repeat itself. Yet, cross-sectional surveys are not only used to capture one-time events. To the contrary, they are quite frequently used by researchers to tap into all types of research questions. Because, it is logistically complicated, time-consuming, and costly to conduct the same study at regular intervals with or without the same individuals, cross-sectional studies are frequently the fall-back option for many researchers. In many instances, the use of cross-sectional surveys can be justified from a theoretical perspective; frequently, a cross-sectional study still allows researchers to draw inferences about relationships between independent and dependent variables (Behnke et al. 2006: 70 f.).

However, it is worth noting that the use of these types of surveys to detect empirical relationships can be tricky. Most importantly, because we only have data at one point for both independent and dependent variables, cross-sectional surveys cannot establish causality (i.e., they cannot establish that a change in the independent variable precedes a change in the dependent variable) (De Vaus 2001: 51). Therefore, it is important that findings/conclusions derived from cross-sectional studies are supported by theory, logic, and/or intuition (Frees 2004: 286). In other words, a researcher should only use cross-sectional data to test theories, if the temporal chain between independent and dependent variable is rather clear a priori.

If we have clear theoretical assumptions about a relationship, a cross-sectional survey can provide a good tool to test hypotheses. For example, a cross-sectional survey could be appropriate to test the linkage between formal education and casting a ballot at elections, as there is a strong theoretical argument in favor of the proposition that higher formal education will increase somebody's propensity to vote. According to the resource model of voting (see Brady et al. 1995), higher educated individuals have the material and nonmaterial resources necessary to understand complex political scenarios, as well as the network connections, all of which should render somebody more likely to vote. Vice versa, uneducated individuals lack these resources and are frequently politically disenfranchised. Practically, it is also impossible that the sheer act of voting changes somebody's formal education. Hence, if we analyze a cross-sectional survey on voting and find that more educated individuals are more likely to vote, we can assume that this association reflects an empirical reality. To take another example, if we want to study the influence of age on protesting, data from a cross-sectional survey could be completely appropriate, as well, to study this relationship, as the causal change clearly goes from age to protesting and not the other way round. By definition, the fact that I protest does not make me younger or older, at least when we look at somebody's biological age.

Nevertheless, empirical relationships are not always that clear-cut. Rather contrary, sometimes it is tricky to derive causal explanations from cross-sectional studies. To highlight this dilemma, let us take an example from American Politics and look at the relationship between watching *Fox News* and voting for Donald Trump. For one, it makes theoretical sense that watching *Fox News* in the United States increases somebody's likelihood to vote for Donald Trump in the Presidential Election, because this TV chain supports this populist leader. Yet, the causal or correlational chain could also go the other way round. In other words, it might also be that somebody, who decided to vote for Trump, is actively looking for a news outlet that follows her convictions. As a result, she might watch *Fox News* after voting for Trump.

A slightly different example highlights even clearer that the correlational or causal direction between independent and dependent variable is not always clear. For example take the following example; it is theoretically unclear if the consumption of *Fox News* renders somebody more conservative or if more conservative individuals have a higher likelihood to watch *Fox News*. Rather than one variable influencing the other, both factors might mutually reinforce each other. Therefore, even if a researcher finds support for the hypothesis that watching *Fox News* makes people more conservative, we cannot be sure of the direction of this association because a cross-sectional survey would ask individuals the same question at the same time.[1] Consequently, we cannot detect what comes first: watching *Fox News* or being conservative. Hence, cross-sectional surveys cannot resolve the aforementioned temporal aspect. Rather than a cross-sectional survey, a longitudinal survey would be necessary to determine the causal chain between being conservative and watching *Fox News*. Such a survey, in particular, if it is conducted over many years and if it solicits the same individuals in regular intervals, could tell researchers if respondents first become conservative and then watch *Fox News* or if the relationship is the other way round.

3.5.2 Longitudinal Survey

In contrast to cross-sectional studies, which are conducted once, longitudinal surveys repeat the same survey questions several times. This allows the researchers to analyze changing attitudes or behaviors that occur within the population over time. There are three types of longitudinal surveys: trend studies, cohort studies, and panel studies.

3.5.2.1 Trend Surveys
A trend study, which is frequently also labeled a repeated cross-sectional survey, is a repeated survey that is normally not composed of the same individuals in the different waves. Most of the main international surveys including the *European*

---

[1]In the literature, such reversed causation is often referred to as an endogeneity problem.

Social Survey or the *World Values Survey* are trend studies. The surveys of the different waves are fully or partly comprised of the same questions. As such they allow researchers to detect broad changes in opinions and behaviors over time. Nevertheless, and because the collected data covers different individuals in each wave of the study, the collected data merely allows for conclusions on the aggregate level such as the regional or the national level (Schumann 2012: 113). To highlight, most of the major surveys ask the question: How satisfied are you with how democracy works in your country? Frequently, the answer choices range from 0 or not satisfied at all to 10 or very satisfied. Since, citizens answer these questions every 2 years, researchers can track satisfaction rates with democracy over a longer period such as 10 years. Comparing the answers for several waves, a researcher can also establish if the same or different independent variables (e.g., unemployment or economic insecurity, gender, age, or income) trigger higher rates of dissatisfaction with democracy. However, what such a question/study cannot do is to track down what altered an individual's assessment of the state of democracy in her country. Rather, it only allows researchers to draw conclusions on the macro- or aggregate level.

3.5.2.2 Cohort Surveys

While trend studies normally focus on the whole population, cohort studies merely focus on a segment of the population. One common feature of a cohort study is that a central event or feature occurred approximately at the same time to all members of the group. Most common are birth cohorts. In that case, birth is the special event that took place in the same year or in the same years for all members of the cohort (e.g., all Americans who were born in or after 1960). Analogous to trend studies, cohort studies use the same questions in several waves. In each wave, a sample is drawn from the cohort. This implies that the population remains the same over time, whereas the individuals in the sample change. A typical example of cohort studies is the "British National Child Study" (NCDS). In the course of this study, 11,400 British citizens born between March 3 and 9, 1958, were examined with respect to their health, education, income, and attitudes in eight waves in a time span of 50 years (Schnell et al. 2011: 237 f.).

3.5.2.3 Panel Surveys

Panel studies normally ask the same questions to the same people in subsequent waves. These types of surveys are the most costly and most difficult to implement, but they are the best suited to detect causal relationships or changes in individual behavior. For example, a researcher could ask questions on the consumption of Fox News and being conservative to the same individual over the period of several years. This could help her detect the temporal chain in the relationship between a certain type of news consumption and political ideologies. Panel studies frequently have the problem of high attrition or mortality rates. In other words, people drop out during waves for multiple reasons, for example, they could move, become sick, or simply refuse further participation. Hence, it is likely that a sample that was representative from the outset becomes less and less representative for subsequent waves of the panel. To highlight, imagine that a researcher is conducting a panel on citizens' preference on which electoral system should be used in a country, and they ask this question every 2 years to the same individuals. Individuals who are interested in electoral politics, and/or have a strong opinion in favor of one or the other type of electoral system, might have a higher likelihood to stay in the sample than citizens who do not care. In contrast, those who are less interested will no longer participate in future waves. Others, like old-age citizens, might die or move into an old people's home. A third group such as diplomats and consultants is more likely to move than manual workers. It is possible to continue the list. Therefore, there is the danger that many panels become less representative of the population for any of the waves covered. Nevertheless, in particular, if some representativeness remains in subsequent waves or if the representativeness is not an issue for the research question, panel studies can be a powerful tool to detect causal relationships. An early example of an influential panel study is Butler and Stokes' *Political Change in Britain: Forces Shaping Electoral Choice*. Focusing on political class as the key independent variable for the vote choice for a party, the authors conducted three waves of panels with the same randomly selected electors in the summer 1963, after the general elections 1964 and after the general elections 1966 to determine habitual voting and vote switching. Among others, they find that voting patterns in favor of the three main parties (i.e., the Liberal Party, Labour Party, and the Conservative Party) are more complex to be fully captured by class.

References

Almond, G., & Verba, S. (1963) [1989]. The civic culture: Political attitudes and democracy in five nations. Newbury Park, CA: Sage.

Archer, K., & Berdahl, L. (2011). *Explorations: Conducting empirical research in canadian political science*. Toronto: Oxford University Press.

Behnke, J., Baur, N., & Behnke, N. (2006). *Empirische Methoden der Politikwissenschaft*. Paderborn: Schöningh.

Brady, H. E., Verba, S., & Schlozman, K. L. (1995). Beyond SES: A resource model of political participation. *American Political Science Review, 89*(2), 271–294.

Burnham, P., Lutz, G. L., Grant, W., & Layton-Henry, Z. (2008). *Research methods in politics* (2nd ed.). Basingstoke, Hampshire: Palgrave Macmillan.

Converse, J. M. (2011). *Survey research in the United States: Roots and emergence 1890–1960*. Picataway: Transaction.

De Leeuw, E. D., Hox, J. J., & Dillman, D. A. (2008). The cornerstones of survey research. In E. D. De Leeuw, J. J. Hox, & D. A. Dillman (Eds.), *International handbook of survey methodology*. New York: Lawrence Erlbaum Associates.

De Vaus, D. (2001). *Research design in social research*. London: Sage.

ESS (European Social Survey). (2017). *Source questionnaire*. Retrieved August 7, 2017, from http://www.europeansocialsurvey.org/methodology/ess_methodology/source_questionnaire/

Fowler, F. J. (2009). *Survey research methods* (4th ed.). Thousand Oaks, CA: Sage.

Frees, E. W. (2004). *Longitudinal and panel data: Analysis and applications in the social sciences*. Cambridge: Cambridge University Press.

Hooper, K. (2006). Using William the conqueror's accounting record to assess manorial efficiency: A critical appraisal. *Accounting History, 11*(1), 63–72.

Hurtienne, T., & Kaufmann, G. (2015). *Methodological biases: Inglehart's world value survey and Q methodology*. Berlin: Folhas do NAEA.

Loosveldt, G. (2008). *Face-to-face interviews*. In E. D. De Leeuw, J. J. Hox, & D. A. Dillman (Eds.), *International handbook of survey methodology*. New York: Lawrence Erlbaum Associates.

Petty, W., & Graunt, J. (1899). *The economic writings of Sir William Petty* (Vol. 1). London: University Press.

Putnam, R. D. (2001). *Bowling alone: The collapse and revival of American community*. New York: Simon and Schuster.

Schnell, R., Hill, P. B., & Esser, E. (2011). *Methoden der empirischen Sozialforschung* (9th ed.). München: Oldenbourg.

Schumann, S. (2012). *Repräsentative Umfrage: Praxisorientierte Einführung in empirische Methoden und statistische Analyseverfahren* (6th ed.). München: Oldenbourg.

Willcox, W. F. (1934). Note on the chronology of statistical societies. *Journal of the American Statistical Association, 29*(188), 418–420.

Wood, E. J. (2003). *Insurgent collective action and civil war in El Salvador*. Cambridge: Cambridge University Press.

Further Reading

Why Do We Need Survey Research?

Converse, J. M. (2017). Survey research in the United States: Roots and emergence 1890–1960. New York: Routledge. This book has more of an historical ankle. It tackles the history of survey research in the United States.

Davidov, E., Schmidt, P., & Schwartz, S. H. (2008). Bringing values back in: The adequacy of the European Social Survey to measure values in 20 countries. Public Opinion Quarterly, *72*(3), 420–445. This rather short article highlights the importance of conducting a large pan-European survey to measure European's social and political beliefs.

Schmitt, H., Hobolt, S. B., Popa, S. A., & Teperoglou, E. (2015). European parliament election study 2014, voter study. *GESIS Data Archive, Cologne. ZA5160 Data file Version, 2*(0). The European Voter Study is another important election study that researchers and students can access freely. It provides a comprehensive battery of variables about voting, political preferences, vote choice, demographics, and political and social opinions of the electorate.

Applied Survey Research

Almond, G. A., & Verba, S. (1963). The civic culture: Political attitudes and democracy in five nations. Princeton: Princeton University Press. Almond's and Verba's masterpiece is a seminal work in survey research measuring citizens' political and civic attitudes in key Western democracies. The book is also one of the first books that systematically uses survey research to measure political traits.

Inglehart, R., & Welzel, C. (2005). *Modernization, cultural change, and democracy: The human development sequence*. Cambridge: Cambridge University Press. This is an influential book, which uses data from the World Values Survey to explain modernization as a process that changes individual's values away from traditional and patriarchal values and toward post-materialist values including environmental protection, minority rights, and gender equality.

Constructing a Survey

4

Abstract

This chapter instructs students on how to conduct a survey. Topics covered include question design, question wording, the use of open- and closed-ended questions, measurement, pre-testing, and refining a survey. As part of this chapter, students construct their own survey.

4.1   Question Design

In principle, in a survey a researcher can ask questions about what people think, what they do, what attributes they have, and how much knowledge they have about an issue.

Questions about opinions, attitudes, beliefs, and values—capture what people think about an issue, a person or an event
These questions frequently give respondents some choices in their answers
Example: Do you agree with the following statement? The European Union should create a crisis fund in order to be able to rapidly bail out member countries, when they are in financial difficulties. (Possible answer choices: Agree, partly agree, partly disagree, and do not agree)
Questions about individual behavior—capture what people do
Example: Did you vote in the last election? (Possible answer choices, yes or no)
Questions about attributes—what are peoples' characteristics
Example: age, gender, etc.
Example: What is your gender? (Possible answers, male, female, no answer)
Questions about knowledge—how much people know about political, social, or cultural issues
Example: In your opinion, how much of its annual GDP per capita does Germany attribute toward development aid?

© Springer International Publishing AG 2019
D. Stockemer, *Quantitative Methods for the Social Sciences*,
https://doi.org/10.1007/978-3-319-99118-4_4

4.2   Ordering of Questions

There are some general guidelines for constructing surveys that make it easy for participants to respond.

1. The ordering of questions should be logical to the respondents and flow smoothly from one question to the next. As a general rule, questions should go from general to specific, impersonal to personal, and easy to difficult.
2. Questions related to the same issue should be grouped together. For example, if a survey captures different forms of political participation, questions capturing voting, partaking in demonstrations, boycotting, and signing petitions should be grouped together. Ideally, the questions could also go from conventional political participation to unconventional political participation. The same applies to other sorts of common issues such as opinions about related subjects (e.g., satisfaction with the government's economic, social, and foreign policy, respectively). Consequently, it makes sense to divide the questionnaire in different sections, each of which should begin with a short introductory sentence. However, while it makes sense to cluster questions by theme, there should not be too many similar questions, with similar measurements either. In particular, the so-called consistency bias might come into play, if there are too many similar questions. Cognitively, some respondents wish to appear consistent in the way they answer the questions, in particular if these questions look alike. To mitigate the consistency bias effects, it is useful to switch up the questions and do not have a row of 20 or 30 questions that are openly interrelated and use the same scale (Weisberg et al. 1996: 89 f.).

4.3   Number of Questions

Researchers always have to draw a fine line between the exhaustiveness and the parsimony of the questionnaire. They want to ask as many questions as are necessary to capture the dependent and all necessary independent variables in the research project. Yet, they do not want to ask too many questions either, because the more questions that are included in an interview or a survey, the less likely people are to finish a face-to-face or phone interview or to return a completed paper or online questionnaire. There are no strict provisions for the length of a survey, though. The general rule that guides the construction of a research could also guide the construction of a questionnaire; a questionnaire should include as many questions as necessary and as few questions as possible.

4.4   Getting the Questions Right

When writing surveys, researchers normally follow some simple rules. The question wording needs to be clear, simple, and precise. In other words, questions need to be written so that respondents understand their meaning right away. In contrast, poorly written questions lead to ambiguity and misunderstandings and can lead to untrust-worthy answers. In particular, vague questions, biased/value-laden questions, threat-ening questions, complex questions, negative questions, and pointless questions should be avoided.

4.4.1 Vague Questions

Vague questions are questions that do not clearly communicate to the respondent what the question is actually all about. For example, a question like "Taken alto-gether, how happy are you with Chancellor Merkel?" is unclear. It is imprecise because the respondent does not know what substantive area the questions is based on. Does the pollster want to know whether the respondent is "happy" with her rhetorical style, her appearance, her leadership style or her government's record, or all of the above? Also the word happy should be avoided because it is at least somewhat value laden. Hence, the researcher should refine her research question by specifying a policy area and a measurement scale and by using more neutral- and less colloquial language. Hence a better question would be: Overall, how would you rate the performance of Chancellor Merkel in the domain of refugee policy during the refugee crisis in 2015 on a 0–100 scale?

4.4.2 Biased or Value-Laden Questions

Biased or value-laden questions are questions that predispose individuals to answer a question in a certain way. These questions are not formulated in a neutral way. Rather, they use strong normative words. Consider, for example, the question: On a scale from 0 to 100, how evil do you think the German Christian Democratic Union (CDU) is? This question is clearly inappropriate for a survey as it bears judgement on the question subject. Therefore a better formulation of the same question would be: On scale from 1 to 100 how would you rate the performance of the Christian Democratic Union in the past year? Ideally, the pollster could also add a policy area to this question.

4.4.3 Threatening Questions

Threating questions might render respondents to surveys uneasy and/or make it hard for the respondent to answer to her best capacities. For instance, the question: "Do you have enough knowledge about German politics to recall the political program of the four parties the Christian Democrats, the Social Democrats, the Green Party, and the Party of Democratic Socialism?" might create several forms of uneasiness on the beholder. The person surveyed might question their capability to answer the ques-tion, they might assume that the pollster is judging them, and they might not know how to answer the question, because it is completely unclear what enough knowledge means. Also, it might be better to reduce the question to one party, because citizens might know a lot about one party program and relatively few things about another program. A better question would be: On a scale from 0 to 100, how familiar are you with the political programs of the Social Democratic Party for the General Election 2017. (0 means I am not familiar at all and 100 means I am an expert.)

4.4.4   Complex Questions

Researchers should avoid complex questions that ask the polled about various issues at once. For example, a question like this: "On a scale from 1 to 10, please rate, for each of the 12 categories listed below, your level of knowledge, confidence, and experience" should be avoided, as it confuses respondents and makes it impossible for the respondent to answer precisely. Rather than clustering many items at once, the researcher should ask one question per topic.

4.4.5   Negative Questions

The usage of negative questions might induce bias or normative connotation into a question. A question such as "On a scale from 0 to 100 how unfit do you think American President Donald Trump is for the Presidency of the United States?" is more value laden than the same question expressed in positive terms: "On a scale from 0 to 100 how fit do you think American President Donald Trump is for Presidency of the United States?" Using the negative form might also confuse people. Therefore, it is a rule in survey research to avoid the usage of negative wording. This includes the use of words such as "not," "rarely," "never," or words with negative prefixes "in-," "im-," "un-." Therefore, researchers should always ask their questions in a positive fashion.

4.4.6   Pointless Questions

A pointless question is a question that does not allow the researcher or pollster to gain any relevant information. For example, the form I-94 from the US Citizenship and Immigration Services that every foreigner, who enters the United States has to fill out does not make any sense. The form asks any foreigner entering the United States: Have you ever been or are you now involved in espionage or sabotage or in terrorist activities or genocide, or between 1933 and 1945 were you involved, in any way, in persecutions associated with Nazi Germany or its allies? Respondents can circle either yes or no. This question is futile in two ways. First, people involved in any of these illegal activities have no incentive to admit to it; admitting to it would automatically mean that their entry into the United States would be denied. Second, and possibly even more importantly, there remain very few individuals alive who, in theory, could have been involved in illegal activities during the Nazi era. And furthermore, virtually all of those very few individuals who are still alive are probably too old now to travel to the United States.

4.5   Social Desirability

The "social desirability paradigm" refers to a phenomenon that we frequently encounter in social science research: survey respondents are inclined to give socially desirable responses, or responses that make them look good against the background of social norms or common values. The social desirability bias is most prevalent in the field of sensitive self-evaluation questions. Respondents can be inclined to avoid disapproval, embarrassment, or legal consequences and therefore opt for an incorrect answer in a survey. For example, respondents know that voting in elections is a socially desirable act. Hence, they might be tempted to affirm that they have voted in the last presidential or parliamentary election even if they did not. Vice versa, the consumption of hard drugs such as cocaine or ecstasy is a socially undesirable act that is also punishable by law. Consequently, even if the survey is anonymously conducted, a respondent might not admit to consuming hard drugs, even if she does so regularly.

The social desirability construct jeopardizes the validity of a survey as socially undesired responses are underestimated. In a simple survey, it is very difficult for a researcher to detect how much the social desirability bias impacts the given responses. One implicit way of detection would be to check if a respondent answers a number of similar questions in a socially desirable manner. For example, if a researcher asks if respondents have ever speeded, smoked cigarettes, smoked marijuana, cheated with the taxes, or lied to a police officer, and gets negative answers for all five items, there is a possibility that the respondent chose social desirability over honesty. Yet, the researcher a priori cannot detect, whether this cheating with the answers happened and for what questions. The only thing she can do is to treat the answers of this particular questionnaire with care, when analyzing the questionnaire. Another, albeit also imperfect, way to detect socially desirable rather than correct answers is by follow-up questions. For example, a researcher could first ask the question. Did you vote in the last parliamentary election? A follow-up question could then ask the respondent for which party she voted for? This follow-up question could include the do not know category. It is likely that respondents remember for which party they voted, in particularly, if the survey is conducted relatively shortly after the election. This implies that somebody, who indicated that she voted, but does not recall her party choice, might be a candidate for a socially desirable rather than an honest answer for the voting question (see Steenkamp et al. 2010: 200–202; Hoffmann 2014: 7 f.; Van de Vijver and He 2014: 7 for an extensive discussion of the social desirability paradigm).

Not only can social desirability be inherent in attitudinal and behavioral questions, it can also come from outside influences such as from the pollster itself. A famous example of the effect of socially desirable responding was the 1989

Virginia gubernatorial race between the African-American Douglas Wilder and the Caucasian Marshall Coleman. Wilder, who had been ahead in the polls by a comfortable buffer of 4–11%, ended up winning the election merely by the tiny margin of 0.6%. The common explanation for that mismatch between the projected vote margin in polls and the real vote margin was that a number of White respondents interviewed by African-Americans declared their alleged preference for Wilder in order to appear tolerant in the eyes of the African-American interviewer (Krosnick 1999: 44 f.).

4.6   Open-Ended and Closed-Ended Questions

In survey research we normally distinguish between two broad types of questions: open-ended and closed-ended questions. Questionnaires can be open ended and closed ended or can include a mixture of open- and closed-ended questions. The main difference between these types of questions is that open-ended questions allow respondents to come up with their own answers in their own words, while closed-ended questions require them to select an answer from a set of predetermined choices (see Table 4.1 for a juxtaposition between open- and closed-ended questions). An example of an open-ended question would be: "Why did you join the German Christian Democratic Party?" To answer such a question, the person surveyed must describe, in her own words, what factors enticed her to become a member of that specific party and what her thought process was before joining. In contrast, an example of a closed-ended question would be: "Did you partake in a demonstration in the past 12 months?" This question gives respondents two choices—they can either choose the affirmative answer or the negative answer. Of course, not all open-ended questions are qualitative in nature. For example, the question, "how much money did you donate to the Christian Democratic Party's election campaign in 2012" requires a precise number. In fact, all closed- and open-ended questions, either require numerical answers or answers that can relatively easily be converted into a number in order for them to be utilized in quantitative research (see Table 4.1).

In fact, the usage of non-numerical open-ended questions and closed-ended questions frequently follows different logics. Open-ended questions are frequently

Table 4.1 Open-ended versus closed-ended questions

Open-ended questions	Closed-ended questions
No predetermined responses given	Designed to obtain predetermined responses
Respondent is able to answer in his or her own words	Possible answers: yes/no; true/false, scales, values
Useful in exploratory research and to generate hypotheses	Useful in hypotheses testing
Require skills on the part of the researcher in asking the right questions	Easy to count, analyze, and interpret
Answers can lack uniformity and be difficult to analyze	There is the risk that the given question might not include all possible answers

Table 4.2 Response choices for the question how satisfied are you with the economic situation in your country?

Operationalization 1	Scale from 0 to 100 (zero meaning not satisfied at all, 100 meaning very satisfied)
Operationalization 2	Scale from 0 to 10 (zero meaning not satisfied at all, 10 meaning very satisfied)
Operationalization 3	5 value scale including the categories very satisfied, satisfied, neutral, not satisfied, not satisfied at all
Operationalization 4	4 value scale including the categories very satisfied, satisfied, not satisfied, not satisfied at all
Operationalization 5	6 value scale including the categories very satisfied, satisfied, neutral, not satisfied, not satisfied at all, and do not know
Operationalization 6	5 value scale including the categories very satisfied, satisfied, not satisfied, not satisfied at all, I do not know

used in more in-depth questionnaires and interviews aiming to generate high-quality data that can help researchers generate hypotheses and/or explain causal mechanisms. Since it can sometimes be tricky to coherently summarize qualitative interview data, qualitative researchers must frequently utilize sophisticated data analytical techniques including refined coding schemes and thought-through document analytical techniques (Seidman 2013; Yin 2015). However, since this is a book about quantitative methods and survey research, I do not discuss qualitative interviewing and coding in detail here. Rather, I focus on quantitative research. Yet, working with a set of categories is not without caveats either; it can lead to biased answers and restrict the respondent in his or her answering possibilities. As a rule, the amount of response choices should not be too restricted to give respondents choices. At the same time, however, the amount of options should not exceed the cognitive capacities of the average respondent either. With regard to a phone or face-to-face interview, there is some consensus that not more than seven response categories should be offered (Schumann 2012: 74).

The choice of the appropriate number of response choices can be a tricky process. As a general rule, it makes sense to be consistent with respect to the selection of response scales for similar questions to prevent confusing the respondent (Weisberg et al. 1996: 98). For example, if a researcher asks in a survey of citizens' satisfaction with the country's economy, the country's government, and the country's police forces, it makes sense to use the same scale for all three questions. However, there are many options I can use. Consider the following question: How satisfied are you with the economic situation in your country? A researcher could use a scale from 0 to 10 or a scale from 0 to 100, both of which would allow respondents to situate themselves. A researcher could also use a graded measure with or without a neutral category and/or a do not know option (for a list of options see Table 4.2). To a certain degree, the chosen operationalization depends on the purpose of the study and the research question but to a certain degree is also a question of taste.

4.7   Types of Closed-Ended Survey Questions

Researchers can choose from a variety of questions including scales, dichotomous questions, and multiple-choice questions. In this section, this book presents the most important types of questions:

4.7.1   Scales

Scales are ubiquitous in social sciences questionnaires. Nearly all opinion-based questions use some sort of scale. An example would be: "Rate your satisfaction with your country's police forces from 0 (not satisfied at all) to 10 (very satisfied)." Many questions tapping into personal attributes use scales, as well [e.g., "how would you rate your personal health?" (0, poor; 1, rather poor; 2, average; 3, rather good; 4, very good)]. Finally, some behavioral questions use scales, as well. For example, you might find the question: "How often do you generally watch the news on TV?" Response options could be not at all (coded 0), rather infrequently (coded 1), sometimes (coded 2), rather frequently (coded 3), and very frequently (coded 4). The most prominent scales are Likert and Guttman scales.

Likert Scale A Likert Scale is the most frequently used ordinal variable in questionnaires (maybe the most frequently used type of questions overall) (Kumar 1999: 129). Likert Scales use fixed choice response formats and are designed to measure attitudes or opinions (Bowling 1997; Burns and Grove 1997). Such a scale assumes that the strength/intensity of the experience is linear, i.e., on a continuum from strongly agree to strongly disagree, and makes the assumption that attitudes can be measured. Respondents may be offered a choice of five to seven or even nine pre-coded responses with the neutral point being neither agree nor disagree (Kumar 1999: 132).

Example 1: Going to War in Iraq Was a Mistake of the Bush Administration
The respondent has five choices: strongly agree, somewhat agree, neither agree nor disagree, somewhat disagree, and strongly disagree.

Example 2: How Often Do You Discuss Politics with Your Peers?
The respondent has five choices: very frequently, frequently, occasionally, rarely, and never.

  In the academic literature, there is a rather intense debate about the usage of the neutral category and the do not know option. This applies to Likert Scales and other survey questions as well. Including a neutral category makes it easier for some people to choose/respond. It might be a safe option, in particular for individuals, who prefer not taking a choice. However, excluding the neutral option forces individuals to take a position, even if they are torn, or really stand in the middle for the precise question at hand (Sapsford 2006; Neuman and Robson 2014). A similar logic applies to the do not know option (see Mondak and Davis 2001; Sturgis et al. 2008). The disadvantage of this option is that many respondents go with "no opinion" just because it is more comfortable. In most cases, respondents choose this option due to conflicting views and not due to a lack of knowledge. So, in a sense, they usually do have an opinion and lean at least slightly to one side or another. That is why the inclusion of a "no opinion" option can reduce the number of respondents who give answers to more complex subjects. On the other hand, if this option is omitted, respondents can feel pressed to pick a side although they really are indifferent, for example, because they know very little about the matter. Pushing respondents to give arbitrary answers can therefore affect the validity and reliability of a survey.

For example, somebody might not be interested in economics and besides getting her monthly paycheck has no idea how the economy functions in her country. Such a person can only take a random guess for this question, if the "do not know" option is not included in the questionnaire. For sure, she could leave out the question, but this might feel challenging. Hence, the respondent might feel compelled to give an answer even if it is just a random guess.

While there is no panacea for avoiding these problems, the researcher must be aware of the difficulty of finding the right number and type of response categories and might think through these categories carefully. A possible way of dealing with this challenge is to generally offer "no opinion" options, but to omit them for items on well-known issues or questions where individuals should have an opinion. For example, if you ask respondents about their self-reported health, there is no reason to assume that respondents do not know how they feel. In contrast, if you ask them knowledge questions (e.g., "who is the president of the European Commission?"), the do not know option is a viable choice, as it is highly possible that politically uninterested citizens do not know who the president of the European Commission is. Alternatively, the researcher can decide to omit the "no opinion" option and test the strength of an attitude through follow-up questions. This way, it might become evident whether the given response represents a real choice rather than a guess (Krosnick 1999: 43 f.; Weisberg et al. 1996: 89 f.). For example, a pollster could first ask an individual about her political knowledge using the categories low, rather low, middle, rather high, and very high. In a second step, she could ask "hard" questions about the function of the political system or the positioning of political parties. These "hard" questions could verify whether the respondent judges her political knowledge level accurately.

The Semantic Differential Scale The use of the semantic differential scale allows for more options than the use of a Likert Scale, which is restricted to four or five categories. Rather than having each category labeled, the semantic scale uses two bipolar adjectives at each end of the question. Semantic differential scales normally range from 7 to 10 response choices (see Tables 4.3 and 4.4).

Large Rating Scales These are scales that have a larger range than 0–10. Such scales can often have a range from 0 to 100. Within this range the respondent is free

Table 4.3 Example of a semantic differential scale with seven response choices

How satisfied are you with the services received?						
1						7
Not at all satisfied						Very satisfied

Table 4.4 Example of a semantic differential scale with ten response choices

Do you think immigrants make your country a better or a worse place to live in?									
1									10
Better place									Worse place

to choose the number that most accurately reflects her opinion. For example, researchers could ask respondents how satisfied they are with the state of the economy in their country, on a scale from 0, not satisfied at all, to 100 very satisfied.

Guttman Scale The Guttman scale represents another rather simple way of measuring ordinal variables. This scale is based on a set of items with which the respondents can agree or disagree. All items refer to the exact same variable. However, they vary in their level of "intensity" which means that even people with low agreement might still agree with the first items (questions with a low degree of intensity usually come first) while it takes high stakes for respondents to agree with the last ones. The respondent's score is the total number of items she agrees with—a high score implies a high degree of agreement with the initial questions. Since, all items of one variable are commonly listed in increasing order according to their intensity, this operationalization is based on the assumption that if a respondent agrees with any one of the asked items, she should have agreed with all previous items too. The following example clarifies the idea of "intensity" in response patterns.

Example: Do You Agree or Disagree that Abortions Should Be Permitted?

1. When the life of the woman is in danger.
2. In the case of incest or rape.
3. When the fetus appears to be unhealthy.
4. When the father does not want to have a baby.
5. When the woman cannot afford to have a baby.
6. Whenever the woman wants.

Due to the Guttman scale's basic assumption, a respondent with a score of 4 agrees with the first four items and disagrees with the last two items. The largest challenge when using a Guttman scale is to find a suitable set of items that (perfectly) match the required response patterns. In other words, there must be graduation between each response category and consensus that agreement to the fourth item is more difficult and restricted than agreement to the third item.

Table 4.5 Example of single-answer multiple-choice question

Who is your favorite politician among the four politicians listed below?		
A	Donald Trump	
B	Emmanuel Macron	
C	Angela Merkel	
D	Theresa May	

Table 4.6 Example of a multiple-answer multiple-choice question

Which medium do you use to get your political information from? (click all that apply)		
A	Television news broadcasts	
B	Radio	
C	Internet	
D	Newspaper	
E	Discussion with friends	
F	Other (please specify)	
G	I do not inform myself politically	

4.7.2   Dichotomous Survey Questions

The dichotomous survey question normally leaves respondents with two answering choices. These two choices can include personal characteristics such as male and female, or they can include questions about personal attributes such as whether somebody is married or not.

Example: Did You Participate in a Lawful Demonstration in the Past 12 Months? (Yes/No)
Please note that some questions that were asked dichotomously for decades have recently been asked in a more trichotomous fashion. The prime example is gender. For decades, survey respondents had two options to designate their gender man or woman, not considering that some individuals might not identify with either of the dichotomous choices. Thus the politically correct way now is to include a third option such as neither nor.

4.7.3   Multiple-Choice Questions

Multiple-choice questions are another form of a frequently used question type. They are easy to use, respond to, and analyze. The different categories the respondents can choose from must be mutually exclusive. Multiple-choice questions can be both single answer (i.e., the respondent can only pick one option) and multiple answer (i.e., the respondent can pick several answers) (see Tables 4.5 and 4.6).

One of the weaknesses of some type of multiple-choice questions is that the choice of responses is rather limited and sometimes not final. For example, in

Table 4.7 Example of a categorical survey question with five choices

Which category best describes your age?	
	Younger than 18
	19–34
	35–50
	51–64
	65 and higher

Table 4.8 Example of a categorical survey question with six choices

In which bracket does your net income fall?	
	Lower than $20,000
	$20,000–$39,999
	$40,000–$59,999
	$60,000–$79,999
	$80,000–$99,999
	Over 100,000

Table 4.6, somebody could receive her political information from weekly magazines, talk shows, or political parties. In the current example, we have not included these options for parsimony reasons. Yet, the option E (other) allows respondents to add other items, thus allowing for greater inclusivity. (But please note that if the respondents list too many options under the category "other," the analysis of the survey becomes more complicated).

4.7.4 Numerical Continuous Questions

Numerical continuous questions ask respondents a question that in principle allows the respondent to choose from an infinite number of response choices. Examples would be questions that ask: what is your age? What is your net income?

4.7.5 Categorical Survey Questions

Frequently, researchers split continuous numerical questions into categories. These categories frequently correspond to established categories in the literature. For example, instead of asking what your age is, you could provide age brackets distinguishing young individuals (i.e., 18 and younger), rather young individuals (19–34), middle-aged individuals (35–50), rather old individuals (51–64), and old individuals (65 and higher) (see Table 4.7). The same might apply to income. For example, we could have income brackets for every $20,000 (see Table 4.8).

Using brackets or categories might be particularly helpful for features, where respondents do not want to reveal the exact number. For example, some respondents might not want to reveal their exact age. The same might apply to income. If they are

Table 4.9 Example of a rank order question

Consecutively rank the following five parties from most popular (coded 1) to least popular (coded 5)	
	Christian Democratic Party
	Social Democratic Party
	Free Democratic Party
	Green Party
	Left Party
	Alternative for Germany

Table 4.10 Example of a matrix table question

How would you rate the following attributes of President Trump?	Well below average	Below average	Average	Above Average	Well above average
Honesty					
Competence					
Trustworthiness					
Charisma					

offered rather broad age or income brackets, they might be more willing to provide an answer than be probed for their exact age or income.

4.7.6 Rank-Order Questions

Sometimes researchers might be interested in rankings. Rank-order questions allow respondents to rank persons, brands, or products based on certain attributes such as the popularity of politicians or the vote choice for parties. In rank-order questions, the respondent must consecutively rank the choices from most favorite to least favorite (see Table 4.9).

4.7.7 Matrix Table Questions

Matrix-level questions are questions in tabular format. They consist of multiple questions with the same response choices. The questions are normally connected to each other, and the response choices frequently follow a scale such as a Likert scale (see Table 4.10).

4.8   Different Variables

Regardless of the type of survey questions, there are four different ways to operationalize survey questions. The four types of variables are string variables, continuous variables (interval variables), ordinal variables, and nominal variables.

A **string variable** is a variable that normally occupies the first column in a dataset. It is a non-numerical variable, which serves as the identifier. Examples are individuals in a study or countries. This variable is normally not part of any analysis.

A **continuous variable** can have, in theory, an infinite number of observations (e.g., age, income). Such a question normally follows from a continuous numerical question. To highlight, personal income levels can in theory have any value between 0 and infinity.

An **interval variable** is a specific type of variable; it is a continuous variable with equal gaps between values. For example, counting the income in steps of thousand would be an interval variable: 1000, 2000, 3000, 4000, . . .

A **nominal variable** is categorized. There is no specific order or value to the categorization (e.g., the order is arbitrary). Because there is no hierarchy in the organization of the data, this type of variable is the most difficult to present in datasets (see discussion under Sect. 4.9.1).

An example of a two-categorical nominal variable would be gender (i.e., men and women). Such a variable is also called **dichotomous** or **dummy** variable.

An example of a categorical variable with more than two categories would be religious affiliation (e.g., Protestant, Catholic, Buddhist, Muslim, etc.)

An **ordinal variable** consists of data that are categorized, and there is a clear order to the categories. Normally all scales are transformed into ordinal variables.

For example, educational experience is a typical variable to be grouped as an ordinal variable. For example, a coding in the following categories could make sense: no elementary school, elementary school graduate, high school graduate, college graduate, Master's degree, and Ph.D.

An ordinal variable can also be a variable that categorizes a variable into set intervals. Such an interval question could be: How much time does it take you to get to work in the morning? Please tick the applicable category (see Table 4.11).

What is important for such an ordinal coding of a continuous variable is that the intervals are comparable and that there is some type of linear progression.

The most frequent types of ordinal variables are scales. Representative of such scales would be the answer to the question: Please indicate how satisfied you are with Chancellor Merkel's foreign policy on a scale from 1 to 5 (see Table 4.12).

Table 4.11 Ordinal coding of the variable time it takes somebody to go to work

Less than 10 min	10-30 min	30-60 min	More than 60 min

Table 4.12 Ordinal coding of the scaled variable satisfaction with Chancellor Merkel

1 not satisfied at all	2	3	4	5 very satisfied

4.9   Coding of Different Variables in a Dataset

Except for string variables, question responses need to be transformed into numbers to be useful for data analytical purposes. Table 4.13 highlights some rules how this is normally done:

1. In the first column in Table 4.13, we have a string variable. This first variable identifies the participants of the study. In a real scientific study, the researcher would render the names anonymous and write: student 1, student 2, . . .
2. The second column is dichotomous variable (i.e., a variable with two possible response choices). Whenever researchers have a dichotomous variable, they create two categories labeling the first category 0 and the second category 1. (For any statistical analysis, it does not matter which one of the two categories you code 0 and 1, but, of course, you need to remember your coding to interpret the data correctly later.)
3. Columns three and four are continuous variables representing the self-reported income and self-reported age the respondent has given in the questionnaire.
4. The fourth column captures a three-item ordinal variable asking individuals about their satisfaction with their job. The choices respondents have are low satisfaction (coded 0), medium satisfaction (coded 1), and high satisfaction (coded 2). Normally, ordinal variables are consecutively labeled from 0 or 1 for the lowest category to how ever many categories there are. To code ordinal variables, it is important that categories are mutually exclusive (i.e., one value cannot be in two categories). It is also important that progression between the various categories is linear.

4.9.1   Coding of Nominal Variables

For some analysis such as regression analysis (see Chaps. 8 and 9), non-dichotomous categorical variables (e.g., different religious affiliations) cannot be expressed in any ordered form, because there is no natural progression in their values. For all statistical tests that assume progression between the categories, this causes a problem. To circumvent this problem for these tests, we use dummy variables to express such a variable. The rule for the creation of dummy variables is that I create one dummy variable less than I have categories. For example, if I have four categories, I create

Table 4.13 Representing string, dichotomous, continuous, and ordinal variables in a dataset

Student	Gender	Income	Age	Job satisfaction
John	1	12,954	43	2
Mary	0	33,456	67	1
James	1	98,534	54	0

Table 4.14 Representing a nominal variable in a dataset

	Dummy 1	Dummy 2	Dummy 3
Muslim	0	0	0
Christian	1	0	0
Buddhist	0	1	0
Hindu	0	0	1

three dummy variables, with the first category serving what is called the reference category. In the example in Table 4.14, the Muslim religion is the reference category against which we compare the other religions. (Since this procedure is rather complex, we will discuss the creation of dummy variables in Chap. 5 again.)

4.10 Drafting a Questionnaire: General Information

In real research, the selection of an overarching question guiding the research process and the development of a questionnaire is theory driven. In other words, social science theory should inform researchers' choices of survey questions, and a good survey should respond to a precise theoretically driven research question (Mark 1996: 15f). Yet, for the exercise in this book, where you are supposed to create your own questionnaire, you are not supposed to be an expert in a particular field. Rather, you can use your general interest, knowledge, and intuition to draft a questionnaire. Please also keep in mind that you can use your personal experience to come up with the topic and overarching research question of your sample survey. To highlight, if a researcher has been affected by poverty in his childhood, he might intuitively have an idea about the consequences of child poverty. In her case, it is also likely that she has read about this phenomenon and liked a hypothesis of one of the authors she has read (e.g., that people who suffered from poverty in their childhood are less likely to go to college). Once you have identified a topic and determined the goals and objectives of your study, think about the questions you might want to include in your survey. Locating previously conducted surveys on similar topics might be an additional step enabling you to discover examples of different research designs about the same topic.

When you select the subject of your study, it is important to take the subject's practicability into account, as well. For one, a study on the political participation of university students can be relatively easily carried through by a university professor or a student. On the other hand, studies on human behavior in war situations for instance are very difficult to be carried out (Schnell et al. 2011: 3 f.). Also keep in mind that before thinking about the survey questions, you must have identified dependent, independent, and control variables. You must have a concrete idea how these variables can be measured in your survey. For example, if a researcher wants to explain variation in a student's grades, a student's cumulative grade average is the dependent variable. Possible independent or explanatory variables are the numbers of hours a student studies per week, the level of her class attendance gauged in percent of all classes, her interest in her field of study gauged from 0 not interested at all to 10 very interested, and her general life satisfaction again measured on a 0–10 scale. In addition, she might add questions about the gender, place of residency (city, suburban area, or countryside), and the year of study (i.e., freshman, sophomore, junior, and senior or first, second, third, and fourth year).

4.10.1 Drafting a Questionnaire: A Step-by-Step Approach

1. Think of an interesting social science topic of your choice (be creative), something that is simple enough to ask fellow students or your peers.
2. Specify the dependent variable as a continuous variable.[1]
3. Think of six to eight independent (explanatory) variables which might affect the dependent variable. You should include three types of independent variables: continuous, ordinal, and nominal/dichotomous variables. Do not ask questions that are too sensitive, and do not include open-ended questions.
4. On the question sheet, clearly label your dependent variable and your independent variables.
5. On a separate sheet, add a short explanation where you justify your study topic. Also add several sentences per independent variable where you formulate a hypothesis and very quickly justify your hypothesis. In justifying your hypothesis, you do not need to consult the academic literature. Rather you can use your intuition and knowledge of the work you have already read.
6. If you encounter problems specifying and explaining a hypothesis, the survey question you have chosen might be suboptimal, and you may want to choose another research question.
7. Add a very short introduction to your survey, where you introduce your topic. The example below can serve as a basis when you construct your survey.

---

[1]For data analytical reasons, it is important to specify your dependent variable as a continuous variable, as the statistical techniques, you will learn later frequently require that the dependent variable is continuous.

Sample Questionnaire

Dear participants

This survey is about the money college students spend partying and possible factors that might influence students' partying expenses. Please answer the following questions which will be exclusively used for data analytical purposes in my political science research methods class. If you are not sure about an answer, just give an estimate. All answers will be treated confidentially. I thank you for contributing to our study.

Dependent variable:

- How much money do you spend partying per week?

Independent variables:

- What is your gender?
  Male   Female   (circle one)
- What is your year of study?
  1   2   3   4   5   6 or higher (circle one)
- On average, how many hours do you spend studying per week?
- On average, how many days do you go partying per week?
  1   2   3   4   5 or more (circle one)
- On a scale from 0 to 100, determine how much fun you can have without alcohol (0 meaning you can have a lot of fun, 100 you cannot have fun at all).
- On a scale from 0 to 100, determine the quality of the officially sanctioned free-time activities at your institution (0 meaning they are horrible, 100 meaning they are very good).
- What percent of your tuition do you pay yourself?

4.11   Background Information About the Questionnaire

Study Purpose This research analyzes university students' spending patterns, when they go out to party. This information might be important for university administrations, businesses, and parents. It might also serve as an indication of how serious they take their studies. Finally, it gives us some measurement on how much money students have at their disposal and how they spend it (or at least part of it).

Hypotheses:

H(1): Guys spend more money than girls.

It is highly possible that guys like the bar scene more than girls do. For one, they go there to watch sports events such as soccer games. Additionally, they like to hang out there with friends while having some pints.

H(2): The more advanced students are in their university career, the less money and time they spend going out.

More advanced classes are supposedly getting more difficult than first or second year classes. This would imply that students must spend more time studying and would therefore have less time to go out. This, in turn, would entail that they are unlikely to spend money for partying purposes.

H(3): The more time students spend studying, the less money they spend going out.

The rationale for this hypothesis is that students that study long hours just do not have the time to go out a lot and hence are unlikely to spend a lot of money.

H(4): The more students think they need alcohol to have fun, the more they will spend going out.

Alcohol is expensive, and the more students drink while going out, the more money they will spend at bars and nightclubs.

H(5): The more students think that their university offers them good free time activities, the less money they will spend while going out.

If students spend a lot of their free time participating in university sponsored sports or social clubs, they will not have the time to go to bars or nightclubs frequently. As a result, they will not spend significant amounts of money while going out.

H(6): People that pay their tuition in full or partly will not spend as much money at bars than people that have their tuition paid.

The rationale for this hypothesis is straightforward: students that must pay a significant amount of their tuition do not have a lot of money left to spend at bars and nightclubs.

References

Bowling, A. (1997). *Research methods in health*. Buckingham: Open University Press.

Burns, N., & Grove, S. K. (1997). *The practice of nursing research conduct, critique, & utilization*. Philadelphia: W.B. Saunders.

Hoffmann, A. (2014). *Indirekte Befragungstechniken zur Kontrolle sozialer Erwünschtheit in Umfragen*. Doctoral Thesis, Düsseldorf.

Krosnick, J. A. (1999). *Maximizing questionnaire quality*. In J. P. Robinson, P. R. Shaver, & L. S. Wrightsman (Eds.), *Measures of political attitudes: Volume 2 in measures of social psychological attitudes series*. San Diego: Academic Press.

Kumar, R. (1999). Research methodology: A step-by-step guide for beginners. In E. D. De Leeuw, J. J. Hox, & D. A. Dillman (Eds.), *International handbook of survey methodology*. New York: Lawrence Erlbaum Associates.

Mark, R. (1996). *Research made simple: A handbook for social workers*. Thousand Oaks, CA: Sage.

Mondak, J., & Davis, B. C. (2001). Asked and answered: Knowledge levels when we will not take "don't know" for an answer. *Political Behaviour, 23*(3), 199–224.

Neuman, W. L., & Robson, K. (2014). *Basics of social research*. Toronto: Pearson Canada.

Sapsford, R. (2006). *Survey research*. Thousand Oaks, CA: Sage.

Schnell, R., Hill, P. B., & Esser, E. (2011). *Methoden der empirischen Sozialforschung* (9th ed.). München: Oldenbourg.

Schumann, S. (2012). *Repräsentative Umfrage: Praxisorientierte Einführung in empirische Methoden und statistische Analyseverfahren* (6th ed.). München: Oldenbourg.

Seidman, I. (2013). *Interviewing as qualitative research: A guide for researchers in education and the social sciences*. New York: Teachers College Press.

Steenkamp, J.-B., De Jong, M. G., & Baumgartner, H. (2010). Socially desirable response tendencies in survey research. *Journal of Marketing Research, 47*(2), 199–214.

Sturgis, P., Allum, N., & Smith, P. (2008). An experiment on the measurement of political knowledge in surveys. *Public Opinion Quarterly, 72*(1), 90–102.

Van de Vijver, F. J. R., & He, J. (2014). *Report on social desirability, midpoint and extreme responding in TALIS 2013*. OECD Education Working Papers, No. 107. Paris: OECD.

Weisberg, H. F., Krosnick, J. A., & Bowen, B. D. (1996). *An introduction to survey research, polling, and data analysis* (3rd ed.). Thousand Oaks, CA: Sage.

Yin, R. K. (2015). *Qualitative research from start to finish*. New York: Guilford.

Further Reading

Nuts and Bolts of Survey Research

Nardi, P. M. (2018). *Doing survey research: A guide to quantitative methods*. London: Routledge (Chap. 1; Chap. 4). Chapter 1 of this book provides a nice introduction why we do survey research, why it is important, and what important insights it can bring to the social sciences. Chapter 4 gives a nice introduction into questionnaire developments and the different steps that go into the construction of a survey.

Constructing a Survey

Krosnick, J. A. (2018). Questionnaire design. In The Palgrave handbook of survey research (pp. 439–455). Basingstoke: Palgrave Macmillan. Short and comprehensive summary of the dominant literature into questionnaire design. Good as a first read of the topic.

Saris, W. E., & Gallhofer, I. N. (2014). Design, evaluation, and analysis of questionnaires for survey research. San Francisco: Wiley. A very comprehensive guide into the design of surveys. Among others, the book thoroughly discusses how concepts become questions, how we can come up with response categories for the questions we use, and how to structure questions.

Applied Texts: Question Wording

Lundmark, S., Gilljam, M., & Dahlberg, S. (2015). Measuring generalized trust: An examination of question wording and the number of scale points. Public Opinion Quarterly, 80(1), 26–43. The authors show that the question wording of the general questions about trust in other individuals (i.e. generally speaking, would you say that most people can be trusted?) matters in getting accurate responses.

Conducting a Survey

5

Abstract

When the questionnaire is in its final form, the researcher needs to determine what the sample and what the population of her study is. This chapter first explains both terms and further distinguishes between random, representative, and biased samples. Second, it discusses several sampling techniques such as quota sampling and snowball sampling. Third, it introduces different types of surveys (e.g., face-to-face surveys, telephone surveys, and mail-in or Internet surveys) the author of a survey can use to distribute it. As a practical component, students test their surveys in an empirical setting by soliciting answers from peers. While this procedure does not allow students to get representative or random samples, it nevertheless offers students the possibility to collect their own data, which they can analyze later. At the end of the unit, students are taught how to input their responses into an SPSS or Stata dataset.

5.1 Population and Sample

When the questionnaire is in its final form, the researcher needs to determine what the population of her study is and what type of sample she will take (see Fig. 5.1).

The **population** is the entire group of subjects the researcher wants information on. Normally the researcher or polling firm is not able to interview all units of the population because of the sheer size. To highlight, the United States has over 300 million inhabitants, Germany over 80 million, and France over 65 million. It is logistically and financially impossible to interview the whole population. Therefore, the pollster needs to select a **sample** of the population instead. To do so, she first needs to define a **sampling frame**. A sampling frame consists of all units from which the sample will be drawn. Ideally, the sample frame should be identical to the population or at least closely resemble it. In reality, population and sampling frame frequently differ (Weisberg et al. 1996: 39). For example, let us consider that the

© Springer International Publishing AG 2019

D. Stockemer, *Quantitative Methods for the Social Sciences*,

https://doi.org/10.1007/978-3-319-99118-4_5

Fig. 5.1 Graphical display of
a population and a sample

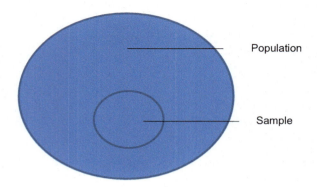

Fig. 5.1 Graphical display of a population and a sample

population are all inhabitants of Berlin. A reasonable sampling frame would include all households in the German capital, from which a random sample could be taken. Using this sample frame, a researcher could then send a questionnaire or survey to these randomly chosen households. However, this sampling frame does not include homeless people; because they do not have a fixed address, they cannot receive the questionnaires. Consequently, this sample drawn from the population will be slightly biased, as it will not include the thousands of people, who live on the streets in Berlin.

A **sample** is a subset of the population the researcher actually examines to gather her data. The collected data on the sample aims at gaining information on the entire population (Bickman and Rog 1998: 102). For example, if the German government wants to know whether individuals favor the introduction of a highway usage fee in Germany, it could ask 1000 people whether or not they agree with this proposal. For this survey, the population is the 82 million habitants of Germany, and the sample is the 1000 people, which the government asks. To make valid inference from a sample for a whole population, the sample should be either representative or random.

5.2   Representative, Random, and Biased Samples

Representative Sample A representative sample is a sample in which the people in the sample have the same characteristics as the people in the population. For example, if a researcher knows that in the population she wishes to study 55% of people are men, 18% are African–Americans, 7% are homeless, and 23% earn more than 100,000 Euros, she should try to match these characteristics in the sample in order to represent the population.

Random Sample In many social settings, it is basically impossible for researchers to match the population characteristics in the sample. Rather than trying any matching technique, researchers can take a random sample. Randomization helps to offset the confounding effects of known and unknown factors by randomly choosing cases. For example, the lottery is a random draw of 6 numbers between

1 and 49. Similarly large-scale international surveys (e.g., the European Social Survey) use randomization techniques to select participants (Nachmias and Nachmias 2008). Ideally, such randomization techniques give every individual in the population the same chance to be selected in the sample.

Biased Sample A biased sample is a sample that is neither representative nor random. Rather than being a snapshot of the population, a biased sample is a sample, whose answers do not reflect the answers we would get had we the possibility to poll the whole population.

There are different forms of biases survey responses can suffer from:

Selection Bias We have selection bias if the sample is not representative of the population it should represent. In other words, a sample is biased if some type of individuals such as middle-class men are overrepresented and other types such as unemployed women are underrepresented. The more this is the case, the more biased the sample becomes, and the potentially more biased the responses will be. Much of the early opinion polls that were conducted in the early twentieth century were biased. For example, the aforementioned Literary Digest poll, which was sent to around ten million people prior to the Presidential Elections 1916 to 1936, was a poll that suffered from serious selection bias. Despite the fact that it correctly predicted the presidential winners of 1916 to 1932 (but it failed to predict the 1936 winner), it did not represent the American voting population accurately. To mail out its questionnaire, *The Literary Digest* used three sources, its own readership, registered automobile users, and registered telephone users. Yet, the readers of *The Literary Digest* were middle- or upper-class individuals and so were automobile and telephone owners. For sure, in the 1910s, 1920s, and 1930s, the use of these sources was probably a convenient way to reach millions of Americans. Nevertheless, the sampling frame failed to reach poor working-class Americans, as well as the unemployed. In particular, during the Great Depression in 1936, rather few Americans could afford the luxuries of reading a literary magazine or owning a car or a telephone. Hence, the unrepresentativeness of *The Literary Digest*'s sample was probably aggravated in 1936. To a large degree, this can explain why *The Literary Digest* survey predicted Alfred Landon to win the presidential election in 1936, whereas in reality Franklin D. Roosevelt won in a landslide amassing 61% of the popular vote. In fact, for *The Literary Digest* poll, the bias was aggravated by non-response bias (Squire 1988).

Non-response Bias Non-response bias occurs, if certain individuals in your sample have a higher likelihood to respond than others and if the responses of those who do not respond would differ considerably from the responses of those who respond. The source of this type of bias is self-selection bias. For most surveys (except for the census in some countries), respondents normally have their entirely free will to decide whether or not to participate in the survey. Naturally, some people are more likely to participate than others are. Most frequently, this self-selection bias stems for the topic of the survey. To highlight, individuals who are politically interested and knowledgeable might be more prone to answer a survey on conventional and unconventional political participation than individuals who could not care less about politics. Yet, non-response bias could also stem from other sources. For example, it could stem from the time that somebody has at her disposal. In addition, persons with a busy professional and private life might simply forget to either fill out or return a survey. In contrast, individuals with more free time might be less likely to forget to fill out the survey; they might also be more thorough in filling it out. Finally, somebody's likelihood to fill out a survey might also be linked to technology (especially for online surveys). For example, not everybody has a smartphone or permanent access to the internet, some people differ in their email security settings, and some people might just not regularly check their emails. This implies that a survey reaches some people of the initial sample, but probably not all of them (especially if it is a survey that was sent out by email).

Response Bias Response bias happens when respondents answer a question misleadingly or untruthfully. The most common form of response bias is the so-called social desirability bias; respondents might try to answer the questions less according to their own convictions but more in an attempt to adhere to social norms (see also Sect. 4.5). For example, social or behavioral surveys (such as the European Social Survey or National Election Studies) frequently suffer from response bias for the simple question whether individuals voted or not. Voting is an act that is socially desirable; a good citizen is expected to vote in an election. When asked the simple question whether or not they voted in the past national, regional, or any other election, citizens know this social convention. Some nonvoters might feel uneasy to admit they did not vote and indicate in the survey that they cast their ballot, even if they did not do so. In fact, over-reporting in election surveys is about 10–15 percentage points in Western democracies (see Zeglovits and Kritzinger 2014). In contrast to the persistent over-reporting of electoral participation, the vote share for radical right-wing parties is frequently under-reported in surveys. Parties like the Front National in France or the Austrian Freedom Party attract voters and followers with their populist, anti-immigration, and anti-elite platforms (Mudde and Kaltwasser 2012). Voting for such a party might involve some negative stigmatization as these parties are shunned by the mainstream political elites, intellectuals, and the media. For these reasons, citizens might feel uneasy divulging their vote decision in a survey. In fact, the real percentage of citizens voting for a radical right-wing party is sometimes twice as high as the self-reported vote choice in election surveys (see: Stockemer 2012).

Response bias also frequently occurs for personality traits and for the description of certain behaviors. For example, when asked, few people are willing to admit that they are lazy or that they chew their fingernails. The same applies to risky and illegal behaviors. Few individuals will openly admit to engage in drug consumption or will indicate in a survey that they have committed a crime.

Biased samples are ubiquitous in the survey research landscape. Nearly any freely accessible survey you find in a magazine or on the Internet has a biased sample. Such a sample is biased because not all the people from the population see the sample, and of those who see it, not everybody will have the same likelihood to respond. In many freely accessible surveys, there is frequently also the likelihood to respond several times. A blatant example of a biased sample would be the National Gun Owner's Action Survey 2018 conducted by the influential US gun lobbyist, the National Rifle Association (NRA). The survey consists of ten value-laden questions about gun rights. For example, in the survey, respondents are asked: should Congress and the states eliminate so-called gun free zones that leave innocent citizens defenseless against terrorists and violent criminals? The anti-gun media claims that most gun owners support mandatory, national gun registration? Do you agree that law-abiding citizens should be forced to submit to mandatory gun registration or else forfeit their guns and their freedom? In addition to these value-laden questions, the sample is mainly restricted to NRA members, gun owners who cherish the second amendment of the American Constitution. Consequently, they will show high opposition toward gun control. Yet, their opinion will certainly not be representative of the American population.

Yet, surveys are not only (ab)used by think tanks and non-governmental organizations to push their demands; in recent times, political parties and candidates also use (online) surveys for political expediency or as a political stunt. For example, after taking office in January 2017, President Trump's campaign sent out an online survey to his supporters entitled "Mainstream Media Accountability Survey." In the introduction the survey directly addressed the American people—"you are our last line of defense against the media's hit jobs. You are our greatest asset in helping our movement deliver the truth to the American people." The questionnaire then asked questions like: "has the mainstream media reported unfairly on our movement?" "Do you believe that the mainstream media does not do their due diligence of fact-checking before publishing stories on the Trump administration?" or "Do you believe that political correctness has created biased news coverage on both illegal immigration and radical Islamic terrorism?" From a survey perspective, Trump's survey is the anti-example of doing survey research. The survey pretends to address the American people, whereas in fact it is only sent to Trump's core supporters. It further uses biased and value-laden questions. The results of such a biased survey is a political stunt that the Trump campaign still uses for political purposes. In fact, with the proliferation of online surveys, with the continued discussion about fake news, and with the ease with which a survey can be created and distributed, there is the latent danger that organizations try to send out surveys less to get a "valid" opinion from a population or clearly defined subgroup of that population, but rather as a stunt to further their cause.

5.3   Sampling Error

For sure, the examples described under biased surveys have high sampling errors, but even with the most sophisticated randomization techniques, we can never have a 100% accurate representation of a population from a sample. Rather, there is always some statistical imprecision in the data. Having a completely random sample would imply that all individuals who are randomly chosen to participate in the survey actually do participate, something that will never happen. The sampling error depicts the degree to which the results derived from a sample differs from the results derived from a population. For a random sample, there is a formula of how to calculate the sampling error (see Sect. 6.6). Basically, the sampling error depends on the number of observations (i.e., the more observations I have in the sample, the more precision there is in the data) and the variability of the data (i.e., how much peoples' opinions differ). For example, if I ask Germans to rate chancellor Merkel's popularity from 0 to 100, I will have a higher sampling error if I ask only 100 instead of 1000 individuals.[1] Similarly, I will have a higher sampling error, if individuals' opinions differ widely rather than being clustered around a specific value. To highlight, if Merkel's popularity values differ considerably—that is, some individuals rate her at 0, others at 100—there is more sampling error than when nearly everybody rates her around 50, because there is just more variation in the data.

5.4   Non-random Sampling Techniques

Large-scale national surveys, measuring the popularity of politicians, citizens' support for a law, or citizens' voting intentions, generally use random sampling techniques. Yet, not all research questions require a random sampling. Sometimes random sampling might not be possible or too expensive. The most common non-probabilistic sampling techniques are convenience sampling, purposive sampling, volunteer sampling, and snowball sampling,

Convenience Sampling Convenience sampling is a type of non-probabilistic sampling technique where people are selected because they are readily available. The primary selection criterion relates to the ease of obtaining a sample. One of the most common examples of convenience sampling is using student volunteers as subjects for research (Battaglia 2008). In fact, college students are probably the most frequently used group in psychological research. For instance, many researchers (e.g., Praino et al. 2013) examining the influence of physical attractiveness on the electoral success of candidates for political office use college students from their local college or university to rank the physical attractiveness of the their study subjects (i.e.,

---

[1]Increasing the number of participants in the sample increases the precision of the data up to a certain number such as 1000 or 2000 participants. Beyond that number, the gains in increasing precision are limited.

political candidates running for office). These students are readily available and cheap to recruit.

Purposive Sampling In purposive sampling subjects are selected because of some characteristics, which the researcher predetermines before the study. Purposive sampling can be very useful in situations where the researcher needs information for a specific target group (e.g., blond women aged 30–40). She can purposefully restrict her sample to the required social group. A common form of purposive sampling is expert sampling. An expert sample is a sample of experts with known and demonstrable expertise in a given area of interest. For example, a researcher uses an expert sampling technique, if she sends out a survey to corruption specialists to ask them about their opinions about the level of corruption in a country (Patton 1990). In fact, most major international corruption indicators such as Transparency International, the World Bank anti-corruption indicator, or the electoral corruption indicators collected by the Electoral Integrity Project are all constructed from expert surveys.

Volunteer Sampling Volunteer sampling is a sampling technique frequently used in psychology or marketing research. In this type of sampling, volunteers are actively searched for or invited to participate. Most of the internet surveys that flood the web also use volunteer sampling. Participants in volunteer samples often have an interest in the topic, or they participate in the survey because they are attracted by the money or the nonfinancial compensation they receive for their participation (Black 1999). Sometimes pollsters also offer a high monetary prize for one or several lucky participants to increase participation. In our daily lives, volunteer surveys are ubiquitous, ranging from airline passenger feedback surveys to surveys about costumer habits and to personal hygiene questionnaires.

Snowball Sampling Snowball sampling is typically employed with populations, which are difficult to access. The snowball sampling technique is relatively straightforward. In the first step, the researcher has to identify one or several individuals of the group she wants to study. She then asks the first respondents if they know others of the same group. By continuing this process, the researcher slowly expands her sample of respondents (Spreen 1992). For example, if a researcher wants to survey homeless people in the district of Kreuzberg in Berlin, she is quite unlikely to find a list with all the people who live in the street. However, if the researcher identifies several homeless people, they are likely to know other individuals that live in the streets, who again might know others.

Quota Sampling As implied in the word, quota sampling is a technique (which is frequently employed in online surveys), where sampling is done according to certain preestablished criteria. For example, many polls have an implicit quota. For example, customer satisfaction polls, membership polls, and readership polls all have an implicit quota. They are restricted to those that have purchased a product or service for customer satisfaction surveys, the members of an organization or party for membership surveys, and the readers of a journal, magazine, or online site for readership polls. Yet, quota sampling can also be deliberately used to increase the representativeness of the sample. For example, let us assume that a researcher wants to know how Americans think about same-sex marriage. Let us further assume that the researcher sets the sample size at 1000 people. Using an online questionnaire, she cannot get a random or fully representative sample, because still not everybody has continuous access to the Internet. Yet, what she can do is to make her sample representative of some characteristics such as gender and region. By setting up quotas, she can do this relatively easily. For example, as regions, she could identify the East, the Midwest, the West, and the South of the United States. For gender, she could split the sample so that she has 50% men and women. This gives her a quota of 125 men and 125 women for each region. Once, she reaches this quota, she closes the survey for this particular cohort (for the technical details on how this works, see also Fluid Survey University 2017). Using such a technique allows researchers to build samples that more or less reflect the population at least when it comes to certain characteristics. While it is cheaper than random sampling, quota sampling with the help of a survey company can still prove rather expensive. For example, using an online quota sampling for a short questionnaire on Germans' knowledge and assessment of the fall of the Berlin Wall in 1989, which I conducted in 2014, I paid $8 per stratified survey. The stratification criteria I used were first gender balance and second the requirement that half the participants must reside in the East of Germany and the other half in the West.

5.5   Different Types of Surveys

Questions about sampling and the means through which a survey is distributed often go hand in hand. Several sampling techniques lend themselves particularly well to one or another distribution medium. In survey research, we distinguish four different ways to conduct a survey: face-to-face surveys, telephone surveys, mail-in surveys, and online surveys.

Face-to-Face Surveys Historically the most commonly employed survey method is the face-to-face survey. In essence, in a face-to-face interview or survey, the interviewer travels to the respondent's location, or the two meet somewhere else. The key feature is the personal interaction between the interviewer who asks questions from a questionnaire and the respondent who answers the interviewer's questions. The direct personal contact is the key difference from a telephone interview, and it comes with both opportunities and risks. One of the greatest advantages is that the interviewer can also examine the interviewee's nonverbal behavior and draw some conclusions from this. She can also immediately respond when problems arise during the task performance; for example, if the respondent does not understand the content of a question, the interviewer can explain the question in more detail.

Therefore, this type of survey is especially suitable when it comes to long surveys on more complex topics, topics where the interviewer must sit down with the respondent to explain certain items. Nevertheless, this type of survey also has its drawbacks: a great risk with this type of survey stems from the impact of the interviewer's physical presence on the respondents' answers. For example, slight differences about the interviewers' ways of presenting an item can influence the responses. In addition, there is the problem of social desirability bias. In particular, in the presence of an interviewer, respondents could feel more pressured to meet social norms than when answering questions. For example, in the presence of a pollster, individuals might be less likely to admit that they have voted for a radical right-wing party or that they support the death penalty. In a more anonymous survey, such as an online survey, the respondents might be more willing to admit socially frowned-upon behaviors or opinions. Face-to-face surveys are still employed for large-scale national surveys such as the census in some countries. Some sampling techniques, such as snowball sampling, also work best with face-to-face surveys.

Telephone Survey In many regards, the telephone interview resembles the face-to-face interview. Rather than personal, the interaction between interviewer and interviewee is via the phone. Trained interviewers can ask the same questions to different respondents in a uniform manner thus fostering precision and accuracy in soliciting responses. The main difference between a telephone interview and a personal interview is logistics. Because the interviewer does not have to travel to the interviewee's residence or meet her in a public location, a larger benefit from this technique is cost. Large-scale telephone surveys significantly simplify the supervision of the interviewers as most or all of them conduct the interviews from the same site. More so than face-to-face surveys, telephone surveys can also take advantage of recent technological advancements. For example, so-called computer-assisted telephone surveys (CATS) allow the interviewer to record the data directly into a computer. This has several advantages: (1) there is no need for any time-consuming transfer process from a transcription medium to a computer (which is a potential source of errors too). (2) The computer can check immediately whether given responses are invalid and change or skip questions depending on former answers. In particular, survey firms use telephone interviews extensively, thus benefiting from the accuracy and time efficiency of modern telephone surveys coupled with modern computer technology (Weisberg et al. 1996: 112–113; Carr and Worth 2001).

Mail-in Survey Mail-in surveys are surveys that are sent to peoples' mailboxes. The key difference between these self-administered questionnaires and the aforementioned methods is the complete absence of an interviewer. The respondent must cope with the questionnaire herself; she only sees the questions and does not hear them; assistance cannot be provided, and there is nobody who can clarify unclear questions or words. For this reason, researchers or survey firms must devote great care when conceiving a mail-in survey. In particular, question wording, the sequence of questions, and the layout of the questionnaire must be easy to understand for respondents (De Leeuw et al. 2008: 239–241). Furthermore, reluctant "respondents" cannot be persuaded by an interviewer to participate in the survey, which results in relatively low response rates. Yet, individuals can take the surveys at their leisure and can think about an answer as much time as they like.

A potential problem of mail-in surveys is the low response rate. Sometimes, only 5, 10, or 20% of the sample sends the questionnaire back, a feature which could render the results biased. To tackle the issue of low response rates, the researcher should consider little incentives for participation (e.g., the chance to win a prize or some compensation for participation), and she should send follow-up mailings to increase the participants' willingness to participate. The upside of the absence of an interviewer is that the researcher does not need to worry about interviewer effects biasing the results. Another advantage of mail-in surveys is the possibility to target participants. Provided that the researcher has demographic information about each household in the population or sample she wants to study, mail-in surveys allow researchers to target the type of individuals she is most interested in. For example, if a researcher wants to study the effect of disability on political participation, she could target only those individuals, who fall under the desired category, people with disabilities, provided she has the addresses of those individuals.

Online Survey Online surveys are essentially a special form of mail in surveys. Instead of sending a questionnaire by mail, researchers send online surveys by email or use a website such as SurveyMonkey to host their questionnaire. Online surveys have become more and more prominent over the past 20 years in research. The main advantage is costs. Thanks to survey sites such as SurveyMonkey or Fluid Survey, everybody can create a survey with little cost. This also implies that the use of online surveys is not restricted to research. To name a few, fashion or sports magazines, political parties, daily newspapers, as well as radio and television broadcasting stations all use online surveys. Most of the time, these surveys are open to the interested reader, and there are no restrictions for participation. Consequently, the answers to such surveys frequently do not cater to the principles of representativeness. Rather, these surveys are based on a quota or convenience sample. Sometimes this poses little problems, as many online surveys target a specific population. For example, it frequently happens to researchers who publish in a scientific journal with publishing houses such as Springer or Tyler and Francis that they receive a questionnaire asking them to rate their level of satisfaction with the publishing experience with the specific publishing house. Despite the fact that the responses to these questionnaires are almost certainly unrepresentative of the whole population of scientists, the feedback they receive might give these publishing houses an idea which authors' services work and which do not work and what they can improve to make the publishing experience more rewarding for authors. Yet, online surveys can also be more problematic. They become particularly problematic if an online sample is drawn from a biased sample to draw inferences beyond the target group (see Sect. 5.2).

5.6   Which Type of Survey Should Researchers Use?

While none of the aforementioned survey types is a priori superior to the others, the type of survey researchers should use depends on several considerations. First, and most importantly, it depends on the purpose of the research and the researcher's priorities. For instance, many surveys, including surveys about voting intentions or the popularity of politicians, nearly by definition require some national random telephone and face-to-face survey or online samples. Second, surveys of a small subset of the population, who are difficult to reach by phone or mail, such as the homeless, similarly require face-to-face interactions. For such a survey, the sample will most likely be a nonrandom snowball or convenience sample. Third, for other surveys more relevant for marketing firms and companies, an online convenience sample might suffice to draw some "valid" inferences about customer satisfaction with a service or a product.

There are some more general guidelines. For one, online surveys can reach a large number of individuals at basically no cost, in particular if there are no quotas involved and if the polling firm has the relevant email addresses or access to a hosting website. One the other hand, face-to-face and telephone interviews can target the respondents more thoroughly. If the response rate is a particularly important consideration, then personal face-to-face surveys or telephone surveys might also be a good choice. The drawback to these types of surveys is the cost; these personal surveys are the most expensive type of survey (with telephone surveys having somewhat lower costs than face-to-face surveys). For research questions where the representativeness or randomness of the sample is less of an issue, or for surveys that target a specific constituency, mail-in or online surveys could be a rather cost-effective means. In particular, the latter are more and more frequently used, because through quota sampling techniques, these surveys can also generate rather representative samples, at least according to some characteristics. However, as the example of the Trump survey illustrates, online surveys can also be used for political expediency. That is why the reader, before believing any of these survey results, in particular, in a nonscientific context, should inform herself about the sampling techniques, and she should look at question wording and the layout of the survey.

5.7   Pre-tests

5.7.1   What Is a Pre-test?

Questionnaire design is complex; hardly any expert can design a perfect questionnaire by just sitting at her desk (Campanelli 2008: 176). Therefore, before beginning the real polling, a researcher should test her questions in an authentic setting to see if the survey as a whole and individual questions make sense and are easily understood by the respondents. To do so, she could conduct the survey with a small subset of the original sample or population aiming to minimize problems before the actual data collection begins (Krosnick and Presser 2010: 266 f.; Krosnick 1999: 50 f.) Such preliminary research or pre-tests make particular sense in five cases.

First, for some questions researchers need to decide upon several possible measurements. For example, for questions using a Likert scale, a pre-test could show if most individuals choose the middle category or the do not know option. If this is the case, researchers might want to consider eliminating these options. In addition, for a question about somebody's income, a pre-test could indicate whether respondents are more comfortable answering a question with set income brackets or if they are willing to reveal their real income.

Second, questions need to be culturally and situationally appropriate, easy to understand, and they must carry the inherent concept's meaning. To highlight, if a researcher conducts a survey with members of a populist radical right-wing party, these members might feel alienated or insulted if she uses the word radical right or populist right. Rather, they define themselves as an alternative that incorporates common sense. Normally, a researcher engaging in this type of research should already know this, but in case she does not, a pre-test can alert her to such specificities allowing her to use situationally appropriate wording.

Third, a pre-test can help a researcher discover if responses to a specific item vary or not. In case there is no variance in the responses to a specific question at all, or very little variance, the researcher could think about omitting the issue to assure that the final questionnaire is solely comprised of discriminative items (items with variance) (Kumar 1999: 132). For example, if a researcher asks the question whether the United States should leave NATO and everybody responds with no, the researcher might consider dropping this question, as there is no variation in answers.

Fourth, a pre-test is particularly helpful if the survey contains open-ended questions and if a coding scheme for these open-ended questions is developed alongside the survey. Regardless of the level of sophistication of the survey, there is always the possibility that unexpected and therefore unclassifiable responses that will be encountered during the survey arise. Conducting a pre-test can reduce this risk.

Fifth, and more practically, a pre-test is especially recommendable if a group of interviewers (with little experience) run the interviews. In this case, the pre-test can be part of the interviewers' training. After the pre-test, the interviewers not only share their experiences and discuss which questions were too vague or ambiguous but also share their experience asking the questions (Behnke et al. 2006: 258 f.).

After the pre-test, several questions might be changed depending on the respondents' reactions (e.g., low response rates) to the initial questionnaire. If significant changes are made in the aftermath of the pre-test, the revised questions should also be retested. This subsequent pre-test allows the researcher to check if the new questions, or the new question wordings, are clearer or if the changes have caused new problems (for more information on pre-testing, see Guyette 1983, pp. 54–55).

5.7.2 How to Conduct a Pre-test?

The creation of a questionnaire/survey is a reiterative process. In a first step, the researcher should check the questions several times to see if there are any uncertain or vague questions, if the question flow is good, and if the layout is clear and appealing. To this end, it also makes sense for the researcher to read the questions aloud so that she can reveal differences between written and spoken language. In a next step, she might run the survey with a friend or colleague. This preliminary testing might already allow the researcher to identify (some) ambiguous or sensitive questions or other problematic aspects in the questionnaire. Then, after this preliminary check, the researcher should conduct a trial or pre-test to verify if the topic of the questionnaire and every single question are well understood by the survey respondents. To conduct such a pre-test, researchers normally choose a handful of individuals who are similar to those that will actually take the survey. When conducting her trial, the researcher must also decide whether the interviewer (if he does not run the pre-test himself) informs the respondent about the purpose of the survey beforehand. An informed respondent could be more aware of the interviewing process and any kinds of issues that arise during the pre-test. However, the flipside is that the respondent may take the survey less seriously. The so-called respondent debriefing session offers a middle way addressing the described obstacles. In a first step, the pre-test is conducted without informing the respondent beforehand. Then, shortly after the end of the pre-test, the interviewer asks the respondent about obstacles and challenges the respondent encountered in the course of the pre-test (Campanelli 2008: 180).

References

Battaglia, M. (2008). Convenience sampling. In P. J. Lavrakas (Ed.), *Encyclopedia of survey research methods*. Thousand Oaks, CA: Sage.

Behnke, J., Baur, N., & Behnke, N. (2006). *Empirische Methoden der Politikwissenschaft*. Paderborn: Schöningh.

Bickman, L., & Rog, D. J. (1998). *Handbook of applied social research methods*. Thousand Oaks, CA: Sage.

Black, T. R. (1999). *Doing quantitative research in the social sciences: An integrated approach to research design, measurement, and statistics*. Thousand Oaks, CA: Sage.

Campanelli, P. (2008). *Testing survey questions*. In E. D. De Leeuw, J. J. Hox, & D. A. Dillman (Eds.), *International handbook of survey methodology*. New York: Lawrence Erlbaum Associates.

Carr, E. C., & Worth, A. (2001). The use of the telephone interview for research. *NT research, 6*(1), 511–524.

De Leeuw, E. D., Hox, J. J., & Dillman, D. A. (2008). Mixed-mode surveys: When and why. In *International handbook of survey methodology* (pp. 299–316). New York: Routledge.

Fluid Surveys University. (2017). *Quota sampling effectively – How to get a representative sample for your online surveys*. Retrieved December 1, 2017, from http://fluidsurveys.com/university/using-quotas-effectively-get-representative-sample-online-surveys/

Guyette, S. (1983). *Community based research: A handbook for native Americans*. Los Angeles: American Indian Studies Center.

Krosnick, J. A. (1999). *Maximizing questionnaire quality.* In J. P. Robinson, P. R. Shaver, & L. S. Wrightsman (Eds.), *Measures of political attitudes: Volume 2 in measures of social psychological attitudes series.* San Diego: Academic Press.

Krosnick, J. A., & Presser, S. (2010). *Question and questionnaire design.* In P. V. Marsden & J. D. Wright (Eds.), *Handbook of survey research.* Bingley: Emerald.

Kumar, R. (1999). Research methodology: A step-by-step guide for beginners. In E. D. De Leeuw, J. J. Hox, & D. A. Dillman (Eds.), *International handbook of survey methodology.* New York: Lawrence Erlbaum Associates.

Mudde, C., & Kaltwasser, C. R. (Eds.). (2012). *Populism in Europe and the Americas: Threat or corrective for democracy.* Cambridge: Cambridge University Press.

Nachmias, C. F., & Nachmias, D. (2008). *Research methods in the social sciences* (7th ed.). New York: Worth.

Patton, M. Q. (1990). *Qualitative evaluation and research methods* (2nd ed.). Newbury Park, CA: Sage.

Praino, R., Stockemer, D., & Moscardelli, V. G. (2013). The lingering effect of scandals in congressional elections: Incumbents, challengers, and voters. *Social Science Quarterly, 94*(4), 1045–1061.

Spreen, M. (1992). Rare populations, hidden populations and link-tracing designs: What and why? *Bulletin Methodologie Sociologique, 36*(1), 34–58.

Squire, P. (1988). Why the 1936 literary digest poll failed. *Public Opinion Quarterly, 52*(1), 125–133.

Stockemer, D. (2012). The Swiss radical right: Who are the (new) voters of Swiss Peoples' Party? *Representation, 48*(2), 197–208.

Weisberg, H. F., Krosnick, J. A., & Bowen, B. D. (1996). *An introduction to survey research, polling, and data analysis* (3rd ed.). Thousand Oaks, CA: Sage.

Zeglovits, E., & Kritzinger, S. (2014). New attempts to reduce overreporting of voter turnout and their effects. *International Journal of Public Opinion Research, 26*(2), 224–234.

Further Reading

Constructing and Conducting a Survey

Kelley, K., Clark, B., Brown, V., & Sitzia, J. (2003). Good practice in the conduct and reporting of survey research. *International Journal for Quality in Health Care, 15*(3), 261–266. The short article provides a hands-on step-by-step approach into data collection, data analysis, and reporting. For each step of the survey process, it identifies best practices and pitfalls to be avoided so that the survey becomes valid and credible.

Krosnick, J. A., Presser, S., Fealing, K. H., Ruggles, S., & Vannette, D. L. (2015). *The future of survey research: Challenges and opportunities.* The National Science Foundation Advisory Committee for the social, behavioral and economic sciences subcommittee on advancing sbe survey research. Available online at: http://www.nsf.gov/sbe/AC_Materials/The_Future_of_Survey_Research.pdf. Comprehensive reports on the best practices, challenges, innovations, and new data-collection strategies in survey research.

Rea, L. M., & Parker, R. A. (2014). *Designing and conducting survey research: A comprehensive guide.* San Francisco: Wiley. A very comprehensive book into survey research consisting of three parts: (1) developing and administering a questionnaire, (2) ensuring scientific accuracy, and (3) presenting and analyzing survey results.

Internet Survey

Alessi, E. J., & Martin, J. I. (2010). Conducting an internet-based survey: Benefits, pitfalls, and lessons learned. *Social Work Research*, *34*(2), 122–128. This text provides a very hands-on introduction into the conduct of an Internet survey with a special focus on recruitment strategies and response rate.

De Bruijne, M., & Wijnant, A. (2014). Improving response rates and questionnaire design for mobile web surveys. *Public Opinion Quarterly*, 78(4), 951–962. This research note provides some practical lessons how the response rate and data quality can be improved for Internet surveys especially constructed for smartphones.

Univariate Statistics

6

Abstract

This first practical chapter is split into two parts. In the first part, I succinctly present the two statistical software packages, SPSS and Stata, which are probably the most used statistical programs in the social sciences. I also explain how to input data into SPSS and Stata datasets. Second, I cover the two univariate statistical categories, frequency tables and descriptive statistics, as well as some graphical representations of a variable (i.e., boxplot, pie chart, and histogram). For each test, the mathematical foundations as well as the practical implementation in SPSS and Stata will be introduced based on the sample survey presented at the end of Chap. 4.

6.1 SPSS and Stata

SPSS and Stata are probably the most frequently used software packages in introductory statistics' classes. Both programs are complete, integrated statistics packages that allow for data analysis, data management, and graphics. They are available in most university libraries and are rather simple to navigate. For each test or graphic, the book will illustrate the logic behind the test, its mathematical foundations, as well as illustrate how to conduct the respective analysis in both SPSS and Stata. Depending on which software package you use, you only need to read either the SPSS or the Stata example.

6.2 Putting Data into an SPSS Spreadsheet

To create a data file in SPSS, open SPSS then click on *new dataset*. This opens up a spreadsheet similar to an Excel document. There are two parts to any SPSS dataset, one part labeled Variable View and one part labeled Data View. Data View is used to enter data. Variable View is used to set up the data—names, variable labels, value

© Springer International Publishing AG 2019

D. Stockemer, *Quantitative Methods for the Social Sciences*,

https://doi.org/10.1007/978-3-319-99118-4_6

File Edit View Data Transform Analyze Direct Marketing Graphs Utilities Add-ons Window Help

	Name	Type	Width	Decimals	Label	Values	Missing	Columns	Align	Measure	Role
1	Student	String	10	0		None	None	10	Left	Nominal	Input
2	Money_Spe...	Numeric	10	2		None	None	16	Right	Scale	Input
3	Study_Time	Numeric	10	0		None	None	8	Right	Scale	Input
4	Gender	Numeric	8	2		None	None	8	Right	Nominal	Input
5	Year	Numeric	10	2		None	None	8	Right	Scale	Input
6	Times_Part...	Numeric	10	2		None	None	12	Right	Scale	Input
7	Fun_Withou...	Numeric	10	2		None	None	14	Right	Scale	Input
8	Quality_Extr...	Numeric	10	2		None	None	24	Right	Scale	Input
9	Amount_Tui...	Numeric	10	2		None	None	12	Right	Scale	Input

Fig. 6.1 Display of the sample data in *Variable View*

File Edit View Data Transform Analyze Direct Marketing Graphs Utilities Add-ons Window Help

10 : Student   Student10

	Student	Money_Spent_Partying	Study_Time	Gender	Year	Times_Partying	Fun_Without_Alcohol	Quality_Extra_Curricular_Activities	Amount_Tuition_Student_Pays
1	Student1	50.00	7	.00	2.00	3.00	60.00	20.00	30.00
2	Student2	35.00	8	1.00	3.00	2.00	70.00	40.00	50.00
3	Student3	120.00	12	1.00	3.00	4.00	30.00	60.00	60.00
4	Student4	80.00	3	.00	4.00	4.00	50.00	70.00	100.00
5	Student5	100.00	11	.00	1.00	1.00	30.00	80.00	.00
6	Student6	120.00	14	1.00	5.00	.00	20.00	40.00	.00
7	Student7	90.00	11	.00	4.00	2.00	50.00	50.00	.00
8	Student8	80.00	10	1.00	4.00	3.00	40.00	50.00	10.00
9	Student9	70.00	9	.00	3.00	3.00	30.00	50.00	60.00
10	Student10	80.00	8	1.00	2.00	3.00	40.00	40.00	100.00
11	Student11	60.00	12	1.00	4.00	2.00	60.00	60.00	.00
12	Student12	50.00	14	1.00	2.00	1.00	30.00	70.00	10.00

Fig. 6.2 Display of the sample data in *Data View*

labels, etc. To change from *Data View* to *Variable View*, click on the icons in the lower left corner of the dataset.

The first step of creating a dataset consists normally of labeling the data. We generally do this labeling in the *Variable View*. In the *Variable View*, each row represents one variable. Each column represents a case such as a person or a country (see Fig. 6.1). The first variable we normally enter into a dataset is a string variable, an identifier of the cases for which we have collected data for. To enter your survey data, go to the *Variable View* and write in "respondent" in the first row of the first column labeled *Name*. If you enter your own data, label these data appropriately. Because this first variable is normally a string variable (i.e., a non-numeric variable), choose the option *String* in the second column. The other variables are normally numeric variables—the actual data. Include their variable names in the subsequent rows, and make sure that these variables are labeled as *Numeric* (i.e., check the second column). When you label the data, make sure that you do not leave any space between letters, as SPSS will not allow you to leave any space.

The copied graph above shows the *Variable View* of the data from our sample questionnaire from Sect. 4.11. The first variable, labeled student, is the identifier variable. The second variable is the dependent variable measuring the amount of money students spend per week while going out. The remaining variables are the independent variables.

Figure 6.2 shows the *Data View* of our sample questionnaire data. The variable in the first column is the identifier. The second column is the dependent variable, the amount of money students spend going out. Variables 3–8 are the independent variables.

6.3   Putting Data into a Stata Spreadsheet

To create a data file, you have to click on the icon displaying a spreadsheet and a pencil 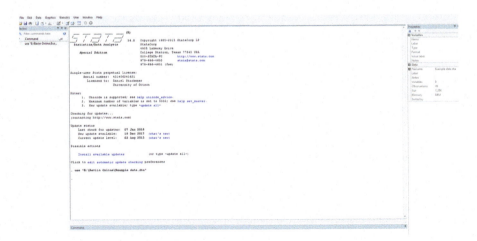 or type "edit" into the command line. This opens up a spreadsheet similar to an Excel document. You can then input the data by hand into this data editor. To do so, you have to first label the data. The first variable we normally enter into a dataset is a string variable, an identifier of the cases for which we have collected data. In our case, this is a string variable, which we label student. Add the name of the other variables in the subsequent fields of the first row. When you label the data, make sure that you do not leave any space between letters, as Stata does not allow you to leave any space. After labeling the variables, you can then input the data. Alternatively, you can enter the data in an Excel spreadsheet and copy it to Stata. When you paste the data into the Stata data editor, Stata asks you whether you want to treat the first row as variable names or data. You click variable names; otherwise, the data will not be labeled.

In Stata we have two different screens, the main screen we use to do our data analysis (see Fig. 6.3) and the data editor or the screen in which we can see the data (see Fig. 6.4). On the main screen, there is some information about Stata and an indication of the dataset you use. On the right side of the screen (i.e., the right upper corner), there is a listing of all the variables. On the bottom of the screen is the command editor, which you will use to do your analyses.

Figure 6.4 shows the data editor featuring our sample questionnaire data. The variable in the first column is the identifier. The second column is the dependent

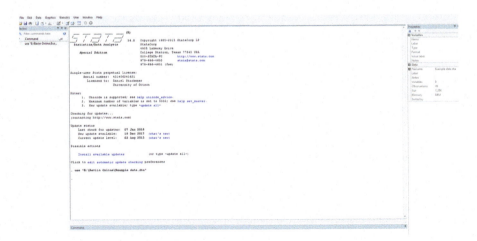

Fig. 6.3 The main Stata screen

Fig. 6.4 Display of the sample data in the Stata data editor

variable, the amount of time students spend per week when partying. Variables 3–8 are the independent variables.

(Please note that when you create your Stata file, some of the original variable names might be too long, and Stata might not accept them. If this is the case, you have to shorten the original name.)

6.4   Frequency Tables

A frequency table is a rather simple univariate statistic that is particularly useful for categorical variables such as ordinal variables that do not have too many categories. For each category or value, such a table indicates the number of times or percentage of times each value occurs. A frequency table normally has four columns. The first column lists the available categories. The second column displays the raw frequency or the number of times a single value occurs. The third column shows the percentage of observations that fall into each category—the basic formula to calculate this percentage is the number of observations in the category divided by the total number of observations. The final column, labeled cumulative percentage, displays the percentage of individuals up to a certain category or point.

Table 6.1 displays a frequency table, of the variable *times partying*. The first column displays the available options (i.e., the six categories ranging from zero to five times and more). The second column shows the raw frequencies (i.e., how many individuals normally party, zero times, once, twice, three times, four times or five times, and more per week). The third column displays the raw frequency in percentages. The final column displays the cumulative percentage. For example, Table 6.1 highlights that 60% of the polled, on average, party two times or fewer per week.

Table 6.1 Frequency table of the variable times partying

On average, how many times per week do you party	Frequency	Percentage	Cumulative percentage
Zero times	3	7.5	7.5
Once	8	20	27.5
Twice	13	32.5	60
Three times	10	25	85
Four times	5	12.5	97.5
Five or more times	1	2.5	100
Total	40	100	

Fig. 6.5 Doing a frequency table in SPSS (first step)

Fig. 6.6 Doing a frequency table in SPSS (second step)

6.4.1 Constructing a Frequency Table in SPSS

Step 1: Go to Analyze—Descriptive Statistics—Frequencies (see Fig. 6.5).
Step 2: Highlight the variable—times_partying—and then click on the arrow. The variable appears in the right rectangle. Then click okay (see Fig. 6.6).

The SPSS output has five columns (see Table 6.2). Columns one, two, three, and five mimic Table 4.6. The first variable is the identifier and displays the existing

Table 6.2   SPSS Frequency table output

Times_Partying

		Frequency	Percent	Valid percent	Cumulative percent
Valid	0.00	3	7.5	7.5	7.5
	1.00	8	20.0	20.0	27.5
	2.00	13	32.5	32.5	60.0
	3.00	10	25.0	25.0	85.0
	4.00	5	12.5	12.5	97.5
	5.00	1	2.5	2.5	100.0
	Total	40	100.0	100.0	

Fig. 6.7 Doing a frequency
table in Stata

Command
tab Times_Partying

categories. Columns two, three, and five display the raw frequency, the corresponding percentage for each category, and the cumulative percentage, respectively. The fourth column, labeled valid percent, displays the percentage of each cell by taking into consideration missing values. Missing values are answers to questions left blank by the respondent (i.e., a respondent did not answer the question). In our example, all survey respondents answered the question on how many times they normally go party. Therefore, there are no missing values, and the values in column four match the values in column three.

6.4.2   Constructing a Frequency Table in Stata

Step 1: Write in the Stata Command field "tab Times_Partying," and press enter.
       (Alternatively, you can also write tab and then click on the variable Times_Partying in the upper right corner of the display.) (See Fig. 6.7.)

The Stata output in Table 6.3 has four columns: (1) variable name (this lists all the possible categories), (2) raw frequency (lists the occurrence of each category), (3) Percent per category (lists the percentage of values that fall into any category), and (4) cumulative percentage (the cumulative percentage of values that fall into the listed category or a lower category).

Table 6.3 Stata frequency table output

Times_Party ing	Freq.	Percent	Cum.
0	3	7.50	7.50
1	8	20.00	27.50
2	10	25.00	52.50
3	9	22.50	75.00
4	8	20.00	95.00
5	2	5.00	100.00
Total	40	100.00	

6.5   The Measures of Central Tendency: Mean, Median, Mode, and Range

This part shortly introduces the most widely used measures of central tendency or univariate statistics: mean, median, mode, and range.

Mean

The mean is the value we commonly call the average. To calculate the mean, sum up all observations, and then divide this sum by the number of subjects or observations.

In statistical language the mean is denoted by $\bar{x}$ an observation is denoted x, and the sample is denoted by n.

The mean in mathematical language:

$$\bar{x} = \frac{x_1 + x_2 + x_3 + \ldots + x_n}{n} = \frac{\sum_{i=1}^{n} x_i}{n}$$

The mean can be strongly influenced by outliers (i.e., observations that fall far from the rest of the data). To highlight, we take a subsample from our sample dataset. For example, the last five values of the variable money spent partying are 60, 60, 90, 70, and 200.

If we calculate the mean, we will get (60 + 60 + 90 + 70 + 200)/5 = 96

We can clearly see that the mean is strongly influenced by the outlier 200. While the first 4 students in our subsample spend between 60 and 90 $/week partying, the last student spends 200 dollars, which is much different from the other values. Without the outlier 200, the mean would be only 70.

Median

The median, or "midpoint," is the middle number of a distribution. It is less sensitive to outliers and therefore a more "resistant" measure of central tendency than the mean. To calculate the median by hand, just line all values up in order and find the middle one (or average of the two middles when n, the number of observations, is even.).

In our example, we would line up the values: 60, 60, **70**, 90, and 200, and the median would be 70.

If we were to calculate the median without the outlier 200, we would again line up the values: 60, 60, 70, and 90. We would then calculate the mean between the two middle values 60 and 70, which is 65.

Mode

The mode is the value that occurs most often in the sample. In cases where there are several values that occur most often, the mode can consist of these several values. Taking our five values again (i.e., 60, 60, 70, 90, 200), the value that appears most often is 60, which is the mode of this subsample.

Range

The range is a measure that provides us with some indication how widely spread our data are. It is calculated by subtracting the highest from the lowest value. In the five-value subsample used above, the range would be 140 (i.e., 200 − 60).

6.6 Displaying Data Graphically: Pie Charts, Boxplots, and Histograms

6.6.1 Pie Charts

A **pie chart**, sometimes also called circle chart, is one way to display a frequency table graphically. The graphic consists of a circle that is divided into slices. Each slice represents one of the variable's categories. The size of each slice is proportional to the frequency of the value. Pie charts can be strong graphical representation of categorical data with few categories. However, the more categories we include into a pie chart the harder it is to succinctly compare categories. It is also rather difficult to compare data across different pie charts. Figure 6.8 displays the pie chart of the variable Times_Partying. We can see that the interpretation is already difficult, as it is already hard to guess from the graph the frequency of each slice. If we take another variable with more categories such as our dependent variable money spent partying (see Fig. 6.9), we see that the categories are basically indistinguishable from each other. Hence, a pie chart is not a good option to display this variable.

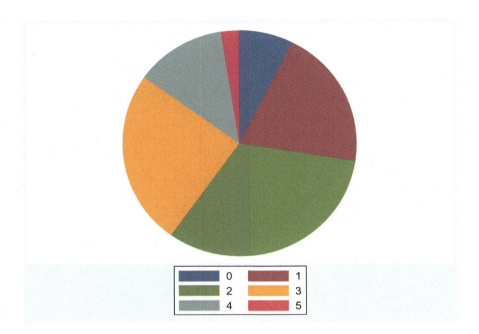

Fig. 6.8 Pie chart of the variable times partying

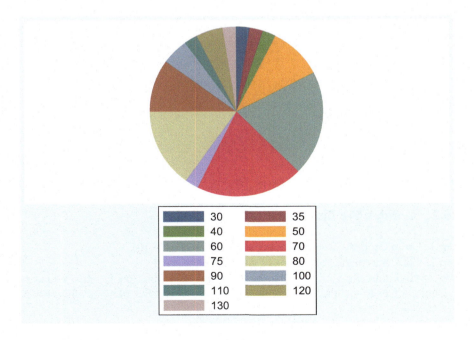

Fig. 6.9 Pie chart of the variable money spent partying

Fig. 6.10 Doing a pie chart in SPSS (first step)

Fig. 6.11 Doing a pie chart in SPSS (second step)

6.6.2 Doing a Pie Chart in SPSS

Step 1: Go to Graphs—Legacy Dialogue – Pie (see Fig. 6.10).

Step 2: Click Summaries of groups of cases (see Fig. 6.11).

Step 3: Highlight the variable—Times_Partying—and click on the arrow next to Define Slices to include the variable in the field. Then click okay (see Fig. 6.12).

Fig. 6.12 Doing a pie chart in SPSS (third step)

The SPSS output in Fig. 6.13 displays the pie chart; in the right-hand upper corner, it denotes the variable name and the existing categories including the corresponding colors in the chart.

6.6.3 Doing a Pie Chart in Stata

Step 1: Write in the Stata Command field: graph pie, over(Times_Partying) (see Fig. 6.14).

Figures 6.8 and 6.9 display the pie chart Stata output of the two variables times partying and money spent partying.

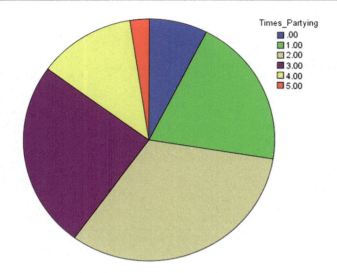

Fig. 6.13 SPSS pie chart output of the variable times partying

```
Command
graph pie, over(Times_Partying)
```

Fig. 6.14 Doing a pie chart in Stata

6.7   Boxplots

A boxplot is a very convenient way of displaying variables. This type of graph allows us to display three measures of central tendency in one graph. The median or the midpoint of each dataset is indicated by the black centerline. The blue/gray shaded box, which is also known as the interquartile range (IQR) includes the mid-50% of the data. The two outer lines denote the range of the data. If values extend up to 1.5 times the interquartile range from the upper or lower boundary of the mid-50%, they are plotted individually as asterisks. These individually plotted values are the outliers.

Figure 6.15 displays the boxplot of the variable average study time. From the graph, we see that the median study time of those students, who participated in the survey, is approximately 10 h. We also learn that the mid-50% of the data generally study between 7 and 11 h/week. The range of the data is 14. (The maximum value denoted by the upper line is 15; the minimum value denoted by the lower line is 1).

Figure 6.16 displays the boxplot of the variable—money spent partying (per week). We see that the median amount of money students spend partying is

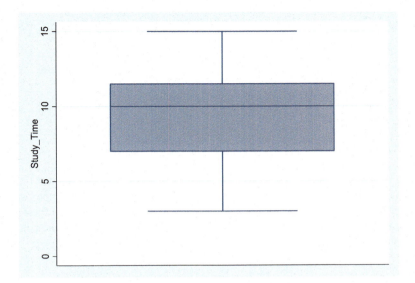

Fig. 6.15 Stata boxplot of the variable study time (per week)

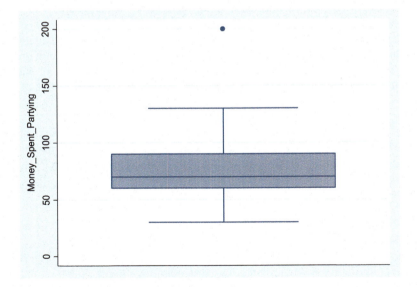

Fig. 6.16 Stata boxplot of the variable money spent partying (per week)

Fig. 6.17 Doing a boxplot in SPSS (first step)

approximately 75 $/week. The mid-50% of students spend between 60 and 90 dollars approximately. At the extremes, students spend 120 dollars at the upper end for partying and 30 dollars at the lower end. The boxplot also indicates that there is one outlying student in the data. By spending 200 dollars, she does not fit the pattern of other students.

6.7.1   Doing a Boxplot in SPSS

Step 1: Go to Graphs—Chart Builder; a dialogue box will open; if this is the case, press okay. You will be directed to the Chart Builder, which you see below (see Fig. 6.17).

Step 2: Go to the item—Choose from—click on Boxplot. Then in the rectangle to the right, three different types of boxplots will appear. Drag the first boxplot image to the open field above. After that, click on your variable of interest—in our case, study time—and drag it to the y-axis. Finally, click okay (see Figs. 6.18 and 6.19).

Figure 6.19 displays the boxplot of the variable study time. The median is at 10 h/ week. The range is 14 h (i.e., the minimum in the sample is 1 h, the maximum is 15 h), and the interquartile range or the mid-50% of the data goes from 7 to 11.

6.7.2   Doing a Boxplot in Stata

Step 1: Write in the Stata Command field: graph box Study_Time (see Fig. 6.20).

Figures 6.15 and 6.16 display two Stata boxplot outputs featuring the variables study time per week and money spent partying per week.

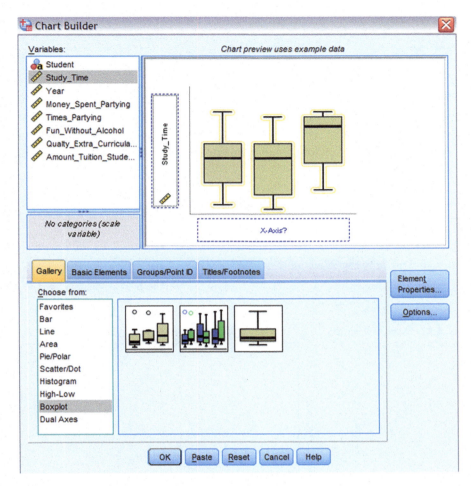

Fig. 6.18 Doing a boxplot in SPSS (second step)

6.8 Histograms

Histograms are one of the most widely used graphs in statistics to graphically display continuous variables. These graphs display the frequency distribution of a given variable. Histograms are very important for statistics in that they tell us if the data is normally distributed. In statistical inference—which means using a sample to generalize about a population—normally distributed data is a prerequisite for many statistical tests (see below), which we use to generalize from a sample toward a population.

Figure 6.21 shows two normal distributions (i.e., the blue line and the red line). In their ideal shape, these distributions have the following features: (1) the mode, mean,

Fig. 6.19 SPSS boxplot of the variable study time (per week)

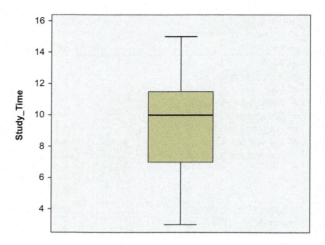

Fig. 6.20 Doing a boxplot in Stata

Fig. 6.21 Shape of a normal distribution

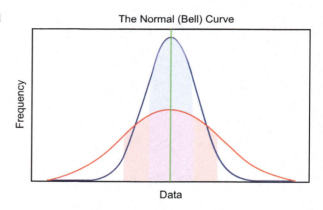

and median are the same value in the center of the distribution. (2) The distribution is symmetrical, that is, it has the same shape on each side of the distribution.

6.8.1 Doing a Histogram in SPSS

Step 1: Go to Graphs—Chart Builder—a dialogue box opens; when this is the case, press okay. You will be directed to the Chart Builder (this is the same procedure as constructing a boxplot).

Step 2: Go to the item "Choose from," and click on Histogram. Then, in the rectangle to the right, four different types of histograms will appear. Drag the first type of

Fig. 6.22 Doing a histogram in SPSS

histogram that appears to the open field above. After that, click on your variable of interest—in our case times spent partying—and drag it to the *x*-axis. Finally, click okay (see Table 7.3 and Fig. 6.22).

The histogram in Fig. 6.23 displays the distribution of the variable money spent partying. We see that the mode is approximately 80 $/month. Pertaining to the normality assumption, we see that the data is very roughly normally distributed. There are fewer observations on the extremes and more observations in the center. However, to be perfectly normally distributed, the bar at 100 should be higher; there should also not be any outlier at 200. However, for analytical purposes, we would

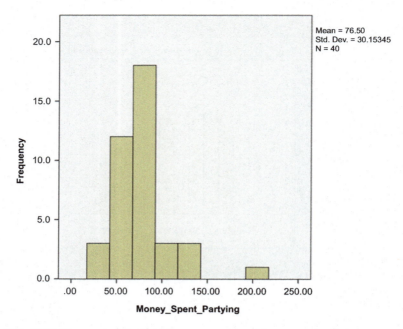

Fig. 6.23 SPSS Histogram of the variable money spent partying per week

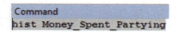

Fig. 6.24 Doing a histogram in Stata

say that this graph is close enough to a normal distribution to make "correct" inferences from samples to populations.

6.8.2   Doing a Histogram in Stata

Step 1: Write in the Stata Command field: hist Money_Spent_Partying (see Fig. 6.24).

The Stata output of the variable money spent partying (see Fig. 6.25) uses somewhat larger bars than the SPSS output and is therefore a little less "precise" than the SPSS output.

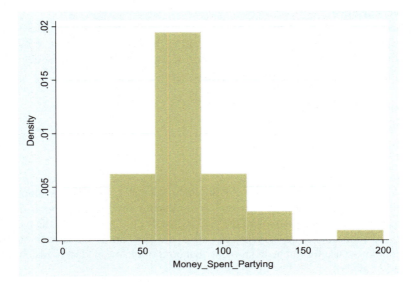

Fig. 6.25 Stata Histogram of the variable money spent partying (per week)

6.9   Deviation, Variance, Standard Deviation, Standard Error, Sampling Error, and Confidence Interval

On the following pages, I will illustrate how you can calculate the sampling error and the confidence interval, two univariate statistics that are of high value for survey research. In order to calculate the sampling error and confidence interval, we have to follow several intermediate steps. We have to calculate the deviation, sample variance, standard deviation, and standard error.

Deviation
Every sample has a sample mean, and for each observation there is a deviation from that mean. The deviation is positive when the observation falls above the mean and negative when the observation falls below the mean. The magnitude of the value reports how different (in the relevant numerical scale) an observation is from the mean.

Formula deviation: Difference between the observation and the mean, $Y_i - \hat{Y}$
Example: Assume we have the following three numbers: 1, 2, and 6
For these numbers the deviations are:
$1 - 3 = -2$
$2 - 3 = -1$
$6 - 3 = 3$
(By definition, the sum of these deviations is 0)

Sample Variance

The variance is the approximate average of the squared deviations. In other words, the variance measures the approximate average of the squared distance between observations and the mean. For this measure, we use squares because the deviations can be negative, and squaring gets rid of the negative sign.

Formula Sample Variance

$$S^2 = \frac{\sum (x_i - x)^2}{n - 1}$$

Standard Deviation

The standard deviation is a measure of volatility that measures the amount of variability or volatility around the mean. The standard deviation is large if there is high volatility in the data and low if the data is closely clustered around the mean. In other words, the smaller the standard deviation, the less "error" we have in our data and the more secure we can be in knowing that our sample mean closely matches our population mean.

Formula Standard Deviation

$$S = \sqrt{\frac{\sum_{i=1}^{N} (x_i - \bar{x})^2}{N - 1}}$$

The standard deviation is also important for standardizing variables. If the data are normally distributed (i.e., they follow a bell-shaped curve), the data have the following properties. Sixty-eight percent of the cases fall within one standard deviation, 95% of the cases fall between two standard deviations, and 99.7% cases fall between three standard deviations (see Figs. 6.26).

Fig. 6.26 Standard deviation in a normal distribution

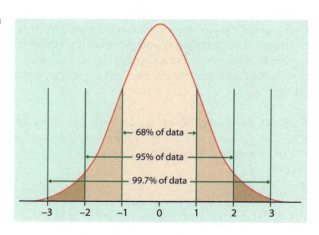

Standard Error

The standard error allows researchers to measure how close the mean of the sample is to the population mean.

Formula of the Standard Error

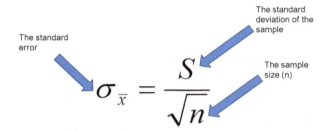

The standard error is important, because it allows researchers to calculate the confidence interval. The confidence interval, in turn, allows researchers to make inferences from the sample mean toward the population mean. It allows researchers to calculate the population mean based on the sample mean. In other words, it gives us a range in which the real mean falls.

(In reality, this method only works if we have a random sample and a normally distributed variable.)

Formula of the Confidence Interval

The confidence interval applied:

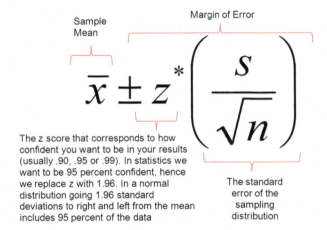

Surveys generally use the confidence interval to depict the accuracy of their predictions.

For example, a 2006 opinion poll of 1000 randomly selected Americans aged 18–24 conducted by the Roper Public Affairs Division and National Geographic finds that:

- Sixty-three percent of young adults ages 18–24 cannot find Iraq on a map of the Middle East.
- Eighty-eight percent of young adults ages 18–24 cannot find Afghanistan on a map of Asia.

At the end of the survey, we find the stipulation that the results of this survey are accurate at the 95% confidence level ±3% points (margin of error ±3%).

This means that we are 95% confident that the *true population* statistic, i.e., the *true* percentage of American youths who cannot find Iraq on a map is somewhere in between 60 and 66. In other words, the "real" mean in the population is anywhere between ±3% points from the mean. This error range is normally called the margin of error or the **sampling error**. In the Iraqi example, we say we have a sampling error of ±3% points (mean ±3% points) (see Fig. 6.27).

Calculating the Confidence Interval (by Hand)

To give you an idea on how to construct the confidence interval by hand using the ten first values of the variable study time per week of our sample dataset (see Appendix 1).

Step 1: Calculating the mean

$$(7 + 8 + 12 + 3 + 11 + 14 + 11 + 10 + 9 + 8)/10 = 9.3$$

Fig. 6.27 Graphical depiction of the confidence interval

Step 2: Calculating the variance

$$(7 - 9.3)^2 + (8 - 9.3)^2 + (12 - 9.3)^2 + (3 - 9.3)^2 + (11 - 9.3)^2 + (14 - 9.3)^2$$
$$+ (11 - 9.3)^2 + (10 - 9.3)^2 + (9 - 9.3)^2 + (8 - 9.3)/9$$
$$= 9.34$$

Step 3: Calculating the standard deviation

$$\sqrt{9.34} = 3.06$$

Step 4: Calculating the standard error

$$\left(\frac{9.34}{\sqrt{10}}\right) = 2.95$$

Step 5: Calculating the confidence interval

$$9.3 \pm 1.96 \times \left(\frac{9.34}{\sqrt{10}}\right) = 15.09; 3.51$$

Assuming that this sample is random and normally distributed, we would find that the real average study time of students lies between 3.5 and 15.1 h. This confidence interval is large because we have few observations and relatively widespread data.

6.9.1 Calculating the Confidence Interval in SPSS

With the help of SPSS, we can calculate the standard deviation and the standard error. We cannot directly calculate the confidence interval but instead use the SPSS Descriptive Statistics to calculate it by hand (i.e., we have to do the last step by hand).

Step 1: Go to Analyze—Descriptive Statistics—Descriptives (see Fig. 6.28).
Step 2: Once the following window appears, drag the variable study time to the right. Then, click on options. The menu, which you will see to the right, will open. On this menu, you can choose what statistics SPSS will display. Add the option

Fig. 6.28 Calculating the confidence interval in SPSS (first step)

S.E. mean. (The options for Mean, Std. Deviation, Minimum, and Maximum are checked automatically). Click continue and okay (see Fig. 6.29).

You will receive the following SPSS output (see Table 6.4) (please note that this output is based on data for the variable study time from the whole dataset and not only the first ten observations). The output displays the number of observations (N), the minimum and maximum value, and the mean, accompanied by its standard error and the standard deviation. If we want to calculate the confidence interval, we have to do it by hand by using the formula introduced above.

The confidence interval for the variable study time is:

Calculating the upper limit: $9.38 + 1.96 \times 0.489$
Calculating the lower limit: $9.38 - 1.96 \times 0.489$

Assuming that the questionnaire data (see appendix) was drawn from a random sample of students that is normally distributed, we could conclude with 95% certainty that the real mean in students' study time would lie between 8.42 and 10.34 h (see Table 6.4).

6.9.2 Calculating the Confidence Interval in Stata

Step 1: Write in the Stata Command field: tabstat Study_Time, stats(mean sd semean min max n) (see Fig. 6.30).

(mean = mean; sd = standard deviation; semean = standard error of the mean; min = minimum; max = maximum; max = maximum; n = number of observations)

Fig. 6.29 Calculating the confidence interval in SPSS (second step)

The stat output provides five statistics: (1) the number of observation the calculations are based on, (2) the sample mean, (3) the standard deviation, (4) the minimum sample value, and (5) the maximum sample value. The confidence interval is not explicitly listed. If we want to calculate it, we can do so by hand (see also Table 6.5):

Table 6.4 Descriptive statistics of the variable study time (SPSS output)

Descriptive statistics

	N	Minimum	Maximum	Mean		Std. deviation
	Statistic	Statistic	Statistic	Statistic	Std. error	Statistic
Study_Time	40	3	15	9.38	0.489	3.094
Valid N (listwise)	40					

```
Command
tabstat Study_Time, stats(mean sd semean min max n)
```

Fig. 6.30 Calculating the confidence interval in Stata

Table 6.5 Descriptive statistics of the variable study time (Stata output)

variable	mean	sd	se(mean)	min	max	N
Study_Time	9.375	3.094143	.4892269	3	15	40

Calculating the upper limit: $9.38 + 1.96 \times 0.489$
Calculating the lower limit: $9.38 - 1.96 \times 0.489$

Assuming that the questionnaire data (see appendix) would be drawn from a random sample of students that is normally distributed, we could conclude with 95% certainty that the real mean in students' study time would lie between 8.42 and 10.34 h.

Further Reading

SPSS Introductory Books

Cronk, B. C. (2017). *How to use SPSS®: A step-by-step guide to analysis and interpretation.* London: Routledge. Hands-on introduction into the statistical package SPSS designed for beginners. Shows users how to enter data and conduct some rather simple statistical tests.

Green, S. B., & Salkind, N. J. (2016). *Using SPSS for Windows and Macintosh, Books a la Carte.* Upper Saddle River: Pearson. An introduction into SPSS specifically designed for students of the social and political sciences. Guides users through basic SPSS techniques and statistics.

Stata Introductory Books

Mehmetoglu, M., & Jakobsen, T. G. (2016). *Applied statistics using Stata: A guide for the social sciences*. London: Sage. A good applied textbook into regression analysis with plenty of applied examples in Stata.

Pollock III, P. H. (2014). *A Stata® companion to political analysis*. Thousand Oaks: CQ Press. Provides a step-by-step introduction into Stata. It includes plenty of supplementary material such as a sample dataset, more than 50 exercises and customized screenshots.

Univariate and Descriptive Statistics

Park, H. M. (2008). *Univariate analysis and normality test using SAS, Stata, and SPSS*. Technical working paper. The University Information Technology Services (UITS) Center for Statistical and Mathematical Computing, Indiana University. https://scholarworks.iu.edu/dspace/handle/2022/19742. A concise introduction into descriptive statistics and graphical representations of data including a discussion of their underlying statistical assumptions.

Bivariate Statistics with Categorical Variables

7

Abstract

In this part, we will discuss three types of bivariate statistics: first, an independent samples *t*-test measures if two groups of a continuous variable are different from one another; second, an *f*-test or ANOVA measures if several groups of one continuous variable are different from one another; third, a chi-square test gauges whether there are differences in a frequency table (i.e., two-by-two table or two-by-three table). Wherever possible we use money spent partying per week as the dependent variable. For the independent variables, we employ an appropriate explanatory variable from our sample survey.

7.1 Independent Sample *t*-Test

An independent samples *t*-test assesses whether the means of two groups are *statistically* different from each other. To properly conduct such a *t*-test, the following conditions should be met:

(1) The dependent variable should be continuous.
(2) The independent variable should consist of mutually exclusive groups (i.e., be categorical).
(3) All observations should be independent, which means that there should not be any linkage between observations (i.e., there should be no direct influence from one value within one group over other values in this same group).
(4) There should not be many significant outliers (this applies the more the smaller the sample is).
(5) The dependent variable should be more or less normally distributed.
(6) The variances between groups should be similar.

© Springer International Publishing AG 2019
D. Stockemer, *Quantitative Methods for the Social Sciences*,
https://doi.org/10.1007/978-3-319-99118-4_7

Fig. 7.1 The logic of a *t*-test

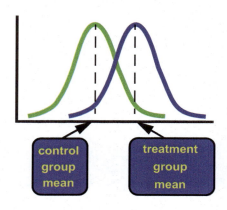

For example, for our data we might be interested whether guys spend more money than girls while partying, and therefore our dependent variable would be money spent partying (per week) and our independent variable gender. We have relative independence of observations as we cannot assume that the money one individual in the sample spends partying directly hinges upon the money another individual in the sample spends partying. From Figs. 6.23 and 6.25, we also know that the variable money spent partying per week is approximately normally distributed. As a preliminary test, we must check if the variance between the two distributions is equal, but a SPSS or Stata test can later help us detect that.

Having verified that our data fit the conditions for a *t*-test, we can now get into the mechanics of conducting such a test. Intuitively, we could first compare the means for the two groups. In other words, we should look at how far the two means are apart from each other. Second, we ought to look at the variability of the data. Pertaining to the variability, we can follow a simple rule; the less there is variability, the less there is overlap in the data, and the more the two groups are distinct. Therefore, to determine whether there is a difference between two groups, two conditions must be met: (1) the two group means must differ quite considerably, and (2) the spread of the two distributions must be relatively low. More precisely, we have to judge the difference between the two means relative to the spread or variability of their scores (see Fig. 7.1). The *t*-test does just this.

Figure 7.2 graphically illustrates that it is not enough that two group means are different from one another. Rather, it is also important how close the values of the two groups cluster around a mean. In the last of the three graphs, we can see that the two groups are distinct (i.e., there is basically no data overlap between the two groups). In the middle graph, we can be rather sure that these two groups are similar (i.e., more than 80% of the data points are indistinguishable; they could belong to either of the two groups). Looking at the first graph, we see that most of the observations clearly belong to one of the two groups but that there is also some overlap. In this case, we would not be sure that the two groups are different.

Fig. 7.2 The question of variability in a *t*-test

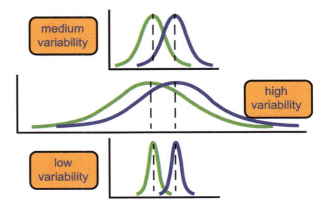

Fig. 7.3 Formula/logic of a *t*-test

Statistical Analysis of the *t*-Test

The difference between the means is the signal, and the bottom part of the formula is the noise, or a measure of variability; the smaller there are differences in the signal and the larger the variability, the harder it is to see the group differences. The logic of a *t*-test can be summarized as follows (see Fig. 7.3):

The top part of the formula is easy to compute—just find the difference between the means. The bottom is a bit more complex; it is called the **standard error of the difference**. To compute it, we have to take the variance for each group and divide it by the number of people in that group. We add these two values and then take their square root. The specific formula is as follows:

$$SE(\bar{X}_T - \bar{X}_C) = \sqrt{\frac{Var_T}{n_T} + \frac{Var_C}{n_C}}$$

The final formula for the *t*-test is the following:

$$t = \frac{\bar{X}_T - \bar{X}_C}{\sqrt{\frac{\text{Var}_T}{n_T} + \frac{\text{Var}_C}{n_C}}}$$

The t-value will be positive if the first mean is larger than the second one and negative if it is smaller. However, for our analysis this does not matter. What matters more is the size of the t-value. Intuitively, we can say that the larger the t-value the higher the chance that two groups are statistically different. A high T-value is triggered by a considerable difference between the two group means and low variability of the data around the two group means. To statistically determine whether the t-value is large enough to conclude that the two groups are statistically different, we need to use a test of significance. A test of significance sets the amount of error, called the alpha level, which we allow our statistical calculation to have. In most social research, the "rule of thumb" is to set the alpha level at 0.05. This means that we allow 5% error. In other words, we want to be 95% certain that a given relationship exists. This implies that, if we were to take 100 samples from the same population, we could get a significant T-value in 95 out of 100 cases.

As you can see from the formula, doing a t-test by hand can be rather complex. Therefore, we have SPSS or Stata to do the work for us.

7.1.1 Doing an Independent Samples t-Test in SPSS

Step 1: Pre-test—Create a histogram to detect whether the dependent variable—money spent partying—is normally distributed (see Sect. 6.8). Despite the outlier (200 $/month), the data is approximately normally distributed, and we can proceed with the independent samples t-test (see Fig. 7.4).

Step 2: Go to Analyze—Compare Means—Independent Samples T-Test (see Fig. 7.5).

Step 2: Put your continuous variable as test variable and your dichotomous variable as grouping variable. In the example that follows, we use our dependent variable—money spent partying from our sample dataset—as the test variable. As the grouping variable, we use the only dichotomous variable in our dataset—gender. After dragging over gender to the grouping field, click on Define Groups and label the grouping variable 1 and 0. Click okay (see Fig. 7.6).

Step 3: Verifying the equal variance assumption—before we conduct and interpret the t-test, we have to verify whether the assumption of equal variance is met. Columns 1 and 2 in Table 7.1 display the Levene test for equal variances, which measures whether the variances or spread of the data is similar between the two groups (in our case between guys and girls). If the f-value is not significant (i.e., the significance level in the second column is larger than 0.05), we do not violate the assumption of equal variances. In this case, it does not matter whether we interpret the upper or the lower row of the output table. However, in our case the significance value in the second column is below 0.05 ($p = 0.018$). This implies that the assumption of equal variances is violated. Yet, this is not dramatic for

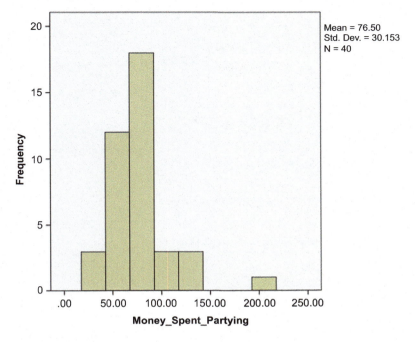

Fig. 7.4 Histogram of the variable money spent partying

Fig. 7.5 Independent samples *t*-test in SPSS (second step)

interpreting the output, as SPSS offers us an adapted *t*-test, which relaxes the assumption of equal variances. This implies that, in order to interpret the *t*-test, we have to use the second row (i.e., the row labeled equal variances not assumed). In our case, it is the outlier that skews the variance, in particular in the girls' group.

Fig. 7.6 Independent samples *t*-test in SPSS (third step)

Table 7.1 SPSS output of an independent samples *t*-test

T-Test

Group Statistics

	Gender	N	Mean	Std. Deviation	Std. Error Mean
Money_Spent_Partying	1.00	21	79.2857	39.18819	8.55156
	.00	19	73.4211	15.63939	3.58792

Independent Samples Test

		Levene's Test for Equality of Variances		t-test for Equality of Means						95% Confidence Interval of the Difference	
		F	Sig.	t	df	Sig. (2-tailed)	Mean Difference	Std. Error Difference		Lower	Upper
Money_Spent_Partying	Equal variances assumed	6.156	.018	.609	38	.546	5.86466	9.62520		-13.62055	25.34987
	Equal variances not assumed			.632	26.740	.533	5.86466	9.27375		-13.17215	24.90147

The significance level determines the alpha level. In our case, the alpha level is superior to 0.05. Hence, we would conclude that the two groups are not different enough to conclude with 95% certainty that there is a difference

7.1.2   Interpreting an Independent Samples *t*-Test SPSS Output

Having tested the data for normality and equal variances, we can now interpret the *t*-test. The *t*-test output provided by SPSS has two components (see Table 7.1): one summary table and one independent samples *t*-test table. The summary table gives us the mean amount of money that girls and guys spent partying. We find that girls (who were coded 1) spend slightly more money when they go out and party compared to guys (which we coded 0). Yet, the difference is rather moderate. On average, girls merely spend 6 dollars more per week than guys. If we further look at the standard deviation, we see that it is rather large, especially for group 1 featuring girls. Yet, this large standard deviation is expected and at least partially triggered by the outlier. Based on these observations, we can take the educated guess that there is, in fact, no significant difference between the two groups. In order to confirm or disprove this conjecture, we have to look at the second output in Table 7.1, in particular the fifth column of the second table (which is the most important field to interpret a *t*-test). It displays the significance or alpha level of the independent samples *t*-test. Assuming that we take the 0.05 benchmark, we cannot reject the null hypothesis with 95% certainty. Hence, we can conclude that there is no statistically significant difference between the two groups.

7.1.3 Reading an SPSS Independent Samples *t*-Test Output Column by Column

Column 3 displays the actual *t*-value. (Large *t*-values normally trigger a difference in the two groups, whereas small *t*-values indicate that the two groups are similar.)

Column 4 displays what is called degrees of freedom (*df*) in statistical language. The degrees of freedom are important for the determination of the significance level in the statistical calculation. For interpretation purposes, they are less important. In short, the *df* are the number of observations that are free to vary. In our case, we have a sample of 40 and we have 2 groups, girls and guys. In order to conduct a *t*-test, we must have at least one girl and one guy in our sample, these two parameters are fixed. The remaining 38 people can then be either guys or girls. This means that we have 2 fixed parameters and 38 free-flying parameters or *df*.

Column 5 displays the significance or alpha level. The significance or alpha level is the most important sample statistic in our interpretation of the *t*-test; it gives us a level certainty about our relationship. We normally use the 95% certainty level in our interpretation of statistics. Hence, we allow 5% error (i.e., a significance level of 0.05). In our example, the significance level is 0.103, which is higher than 0.05. Therefore, we cannot reject the null hypothesis and hence cannot be sure that girls spend more than guys.

Column 6 displays the difference in means between the two groups (i.e., in our example this is the difference in the average amount spent partying between girls and guys, which is 5.86). The difference in means is also the numerator of the *t*-test formula.

Column 7 displays the denominator of the *t*-test, which is the standard error of the difference of the two groups. If we divide the value in column 6 by the value in column 7, we get the *t*-statistic (i.e., $5.86/9.27 = 0.632$).

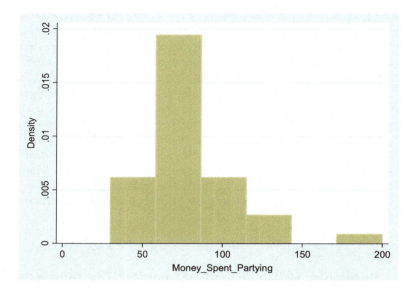

Fig. 7.7 Stata histogram of the variable money spent partying

Command
robvar Money_Spent_Partying, by(Gender)

Fig. 7.8 Levene test of equal variances

Column 8 This final split column gives the confidence interval of the difference between the two groups. Assuming that this sample was randomly taken, we could be confident that the real difference between girls and guys lies between −0.321 and 3.554. Again, these two values confirm that we cannot reject the null hypothesis, because the value 0 is part of the confidence interval.

7.1.4 Doing an Independent Samples *t*-Test in Stata

Step 1: Pre-test—Histogram to detect whether the dependent variable—money spent partying per week—is normally distributed. Despite the outlier (200 $/month), the data is approximately normally distributed, and we can proceed with the independent samples *t*-test (Fig. 7.7).

Step 2: Pre-test—Checking for equal variances—write into the Stata Command field: robvar Money_Spent_Partying, by(Gender) (see Fig. 7.8)—this command will conduct a Levene test of equal variances; if this test turns out to be significant, then the null hypothesis of equal variances must be rejected (to interpret the

Table 7.2   Stata Levene test of equal variances

	Summary of Money_Spent_Partying		
Gender	Mean	Std. Dev.	Freq.
0	73.421053	15.639394	19
1	79.285714	39.188191	21
Total	76.5	30.153454	40

WO = 6.1560718   df(1, 38)   Pr > F = 0.01763701

W50 = 4.4595904   df(1, 38)   Pr > F = 0.04133734

W10 = 5.2486258   df(1, 38)   Pr > F = 0.02760046

Command

```
ttest Money_Spent_Partying, by(Gender) unequal
```

Fig. 7.9   Doing a *t*-test in Stata

Levene test, use the test labeled WO). This is the case in our example (see Table 7.2). The significance level (PR $> F = 0.018$) is below the bar of 0.05.

Step 3: Doing a *t*-test in in Stata—type into the Stata Command field: "ttest Money_Spent_Partying, by(Gender) unequal" (see Fig. 7.9). (Note: if the Levene test for equal variances does not come out significant, you do not need to add equal at the end of the command.)

7.1.5   Interpreting an Independent Samples *t*-Test Stata Output

Having tested the data for normality and equal variances, we can now interpret the *t*-test. The *t*-test output provided by Stata has six columns (see Table 7.3):

Column 1 labels the two groups (in our case group 0 = guys and group 1 = girls).

Column 2 gives the number of observations. In our case, we have 19 guys and 21 girls.

Column 3 displays the mean spending value for the two groups. We find that girls spend slightly more money when they go out and party compared to guys. Yet, the difference is rather moderate. On average, girls merely spend roughly 6 dollars more per week than guys.

Columns 4 and 5 show the standard error and standard deviation, respectively. If we look at both measures, we see that they are rather large, especially for group 1 featuring girls. Yet, this large standard deviation is expected and at least

Table 7.3 Stata independent samples *t*-test output

```
Two-sample t test with unequal variances
```

Group	Obs	Mean	Std. Err.	Std. Dev.	[95% Conf. Interval]	
0	19	73.42105	3.587923	15.63939	65.88311	80.959
1	21	79.28571	8.551564	39.18819	61.44746	97.12396
combined	40	76.5	4.76768	30.15345	66.85646	86.14354
diff		-5.864662	9.27375		-24.90147	13.17215

```
     diff = mean(0) - mean(1)                                        t =  -0.6324
Ho: diff = 0                          Satterthwaite's degrees of freedom =  26.7404

     Ha: diff < 0                       Ha: diff != 0                       Ha: diff > 0
 Pr(T < t) = 0.2663          Pr(|T| > |t|) = 0.5325             Pr(T > t) = 0.7337
```

The significance level determines the alpha level. In our case, the alpha level is superior to .05. Hence, we would conclude that the two groups are not different enough to conclude with 95 percent certainty that there is a difference

partially triggered by the outlier. (Based on these two observations—the two means are relatively close each other and the standard deviation/standard errors are comparatively large—we can take the educated guess that there is no significant difference in the spending patterns of guys and girls when they party.)

Column 6 presents the 95% confidence interval. It highlights that if these data were randomly drawn from a sample of college students, the real mean would fall between 65.88 dollars per week and 80.96 dollars per week for guys (allowing a certainty level of 95%). For girls, the corresponding confidence interval would be between 61.45 dollars per week and 97.12 dollars per week. Because there is some large overlap between the two confidence intervals, we can already conclude that the two groups are not statistically different from zero.

In order to statistically determine via the appropriate test statistic whether the two groups are different, we have to look at the significance level associated with the *t*-

test (see arrow below). The significance level is 0.53, which is above the 0.05 benchmark. Consequently, we cannot reject the null hypothesis with 95% certainty and can conclude that that there is no statistically significant difference between the two groups.

7.1.6   Reporting the Results of an Independent Samples *t*-Test

In Sect. 4.12 we hypothesized that guys like the bar scene more than girls do and are therefore going to spend more money when they go out and party. The independent samples *t*-test disconfirms this hypothesis. On average, it is actually girls who spend slightly more than guys do. However, the difference in average spending (73 dollars for guys and 79 dollars for girls) is not statistically different from zero ($p = 0.53$). Hence, we cannot reject the null hypothesis and can conclude that the spending pattern for partying is similar for the two genders.

7.2   *F*-Test or One-Way ANOVA

T-tests work great with dummy variables, but sometimes we have categorical variables with more than two categories. In cases where we have a continuous variable paired with an ordinal or nominal variable with more than two categories, we use what is called an *f*-test or one-way ANOVA. The logic behind an *f*-test is similar to the logic for a *t*-test. To highlight, if we compare the two graphs in Fig. 7.10, we would probably conclude that the three groups in the second graph are different, while the three groups in the first graph are rather similar (i.e., in the first graph, there is a lot of overlap, whereas in the second graph, there is no overlap, which entails that each value can only be attributed to one distribution).

Fig. 7.10 What makes groups different?

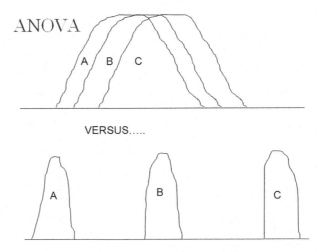

Table 7.4 Within and between variation (as in other occassions, make sure to put the table heading and then the table)

Sample A			Sample B		
• High	Med	Low	High	Med	Low
50	40	30	30	28	12
51	41	31	40	32	18
52	42	32	55	40	30
53	43	33	65	50	45
54	44	34	70	60	55
Mean **52**	**42**	**32**	**52**	**42**	**32**

While the logic of an f-test reflects the logic of a t-test, the calculation of several group means and several measures of variability around the group means becomes more complex in an f-test. To reduce this complexity, an ANOVA test uses a simple method to determine whether there is a difference between several groups. It splits the total variance into two groups: between variance and within variance. The between variance measures the variation between groups, whereas the within variance measures the variation within groups. Whenever the between variation is considerably larger than the within variation, we can say that there are differences within groups. The following example highlights this logic (see Table 7.4).

Let us assume that Table 7.4 depicts two hypothetical samples, which measure the approval ratings of Chancellor Merkel based on social class. In the survey, an approval score of 0 means that respondents are not at all satisfied with her performance as chancellor. In contrast, 100 signifies that individuals are very satisfied with her performance as chancellor. The first sample consists of young people (i.e., 18–25) and the second sample of old people (65 and older). Both samples are split into three categories—high, medium, and low. High stands for higher or upper classes, med stands for medium or middle classes, and low stands for the lower or working classes. We can see that the mean satisfaction ratings for Chancellor Merkel per social strata do not differ between the two samples; that is, the higher classes, on average, rate her at 52, the middle classes at 42, and the lower classes at 32. However, what differs tremendously between the two samples is the variability of the data. In the first sample, the values are very closely clustered around the mean throughout each of the three categories. We can see that there is much more variability between groups than between observations within one group. Hence, we would conclude that the groups are different. In contrast, in sample 2, there is large within-group variation. That is, the values within each group differ much more than the corresponding values between groups. Therefore, we would predict for sample 2 that the three groups are probably not that different, despite the fact that their means are different. Following this logic, the formula for an ANOVA analysis or f-test is **between-group variance/within-group variance**. Since it is too difficult to calculate the between- and within-group variance by hand, we let statistical computer programs do it for us.

File	Edit	View	Data	Transform	Analyze	Direct Marketing	Graphs	Utilities	Ad

Compute Variable...

Programmability Transformation...

Count Values within Cases...

Shift Values...

| 11 : |

	Student		Recode into Same Variables...					Year
10	Student10		Recode into Different Variables...			00		2.00
11	Student11					00		4.00
12	Student12		Automatic Recode...			00		2.00
13	Student13		Create Dummy Variables			00		3.00
14	Student14		Visual Binning			00		3.00

Fig. 7.11 Recoding the variable times partying 1 (first step)

A standard *f*-test or ANOVA analysis illustrates if there are differences between groups or group means, but it does not show which specific group means are different from one another. Yet, in most cases researchers want to know not only that there are some differences but also between which groups the differences lie. So-called multiple comparison tests—basically *t*-tests between the different groups—compare all means against one another and help us detect where the differences lie.

7.2.1   Doing an *f*-Test in SPSS

For our *f*-test we use the variable money spent partying per week as the dependent variable and the categorical variable times partying per week as the factor or grouping variable. Given that we only have 40 observations and given that there should be at least several observations per category to yield valid test results, we will reduce the six categories to three. In more detail, we cluster together no partying and partying once, partying twice and three times, and partying four times and five times and more together. We can create this new variable by hand, or we can also have SPSS do it for us. We will label this variable times partying 1.

Step 1: Creating the variable times partying 1—go to Transform—Recode into Different Variable (see Fig. 7.11).

Step 2: Drag the variable Times_Partying into the middle field—name the Output Variable Times_Partying_1—click on Change—click on Old and New Values (see Fig. 7.12).

Step 3: Include in the Range field the value range that will be clustered together—add the new value in the field labeled New Value—click Add—do this for the all three ranges—once your dialog field looks like the dialog field below click Continue. You will be redirected to the initial screen; click okay and then the new variable will be added to the SPSS dataset (see Fig. 7.13).

Fig. 7.12 Recoding the variable Times Partying 1 (second step)

Fig. 7.13 Recoding the variable Times Partying 1 (third step)

Step 4: For doing the actual *f*-test—go to Analyze—Compare Means—One-Way
     ANOVA (see Fig. 7.14).

Step 5: Put your continuous variable (money spent partying) as Dependent Variable
     and your ordinal variable (times spent partying 1) as Factor. Click okay (see
     Fig. 7.15).

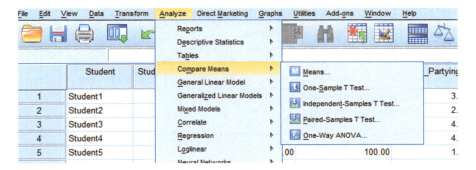

Fig. 7.14 Doing an *f*-test in SPSS (first step)

Fig. 7.15 Doing an *f*-test in SPSS (second step)

7.2.2   Interpreting an SPSS ANOVA Output

The SPSS ANOVA output contains five columns (see Table 7.5). Similar to a *t*-test, the most important column is the significance level (i.e., Sig). It tells us whether there is a difference between at least two out of the however many groups we have. In our example, the significance level is 0.000, which means that we can tell with nearly 100% certainty that at least two groups differ in the money they spent partying per week. Yet, the SPSS ANOVA output does not tell us which groups are different; the only thing it tells us is that at least two groups are different from one another.

In more detail, the different columns are interpreted as follows:

Column 1 displays the sum of squares or the squared deviations for the different variance components (i.e., between-group variance, within-group variance, and total variance).

Table 7.5 SPSS ANOVA output

ANOVA

Money_Spent_Partying

	Sum of Squares	df	Mean Square	F	Sig.
Between Groups	12485.000	2	6242.500	10.053	.000
Within Groups	22975.000	37	620.946		
Total	35460.000	39			

Column 2 displays the degrees of freedom, which allows us to calculate the within and between variance. The formula for these degrees of freedom is number of groups $(k) - 1$ for the between-group estimator and the number of observations $(N) - k$ for within group.

Column 3 shows the between and within variance or sum of squares. According to the f-test formula, we need to divide the between variance by the within variance ($F = 6242.50/620.95 = 10.053$).

Column 4 displays the f-value. The larger the f-value, the more likely it is that at least two groups are statistically different from one another.

Column 5 gives us an alpha level or level of certainty indicating a probability level that there is a difference between at least two groups. In our case, the significance level is 0.000 indicating that we can be nearly be 100% certain that at least two groups differ in, how much money the spent partying per week.

7.2.3 Doing a Post hoc or Multiple Comparison Test in SPSS

The violation of the equal variance assumption (i.e., the distributions around the group means are different for the various groups in the sample) is rather unproblematic for interpreting a one-way ANOVA analysis (Park 2009). Yet, having an equal or unequal variability around the group means is important when doing multiple pairwise comparison tests between means. This assumption needs to be tested before we can do the test:

Step 1: Testing the equal variance assumption—go to the One-Way ANOVA Screen (see step 5 in Sect. 7.2.1)—click on Options—a new screen with options opens— click on Homogeneity of Variance Test (see Fig. 7.16).

Step 2: Press Continue—you will be redirected to the previous screen—press Okay (see Fig. 7.17).

The equality of means test provides a significant result (Sig $= 0.024$) indicating that the variation around the three group means in our sample is not equal. We have to take this inequality of variance in the three distributions into consideration when conducting the multiple comparison test (see Table 7.6).

Fig. 7.16 Doing a post hoc multiple comparison test in SPSS (first step)

Fig. 7.17 Doing a post hoc multiple comparison test in SPSS (second step)

Step 3: Conducting the multiple comparison test—go to the One-Way ANOVA
Command window (see Step 2)—click on the button Post Hoc and choose any of
the four options under the label Equal Variances Not Assumed. Please note if
your equality of variances test did not yield a statistically significant result (i.e. the
sig value is not smaller than 0.05) you should choose any of the options under the
label Equal Variances Assumed) (see Fig. 7.18).

Table 7.6 Robust test of equality of means

Test of Homogeneity of Variances

Money_Spent_Partying

Levene Statistic	df1	df2	Sig.
4.122	2	37	.024

ANOVA

Money_Spent_Partying

	Sum of Squares	df	Mean Square	F	Sig.
Between Groups	12485.000	2	6242.500	10.053	.000
Within Groups	22975.000	37	620.946		
Total	35460.000	39			

Fig. 7.18 Doing a post hoc multiple comparison test in SPSS (third step)

The post hoc multiple comparison test (see Table 7.7) allows us to decipher which groups are actually statistically different from one another. From the SPSS output, we see that individuals who either do not go out not at all or go out once per week (group 0) spend less than individuals who go out four times or more (group 2). The average mean difference is 43 dollars per week, this difference is statistically different from zero ($p = 0.032$). We also see from the SPSS output that individuals who go out and party two or three times (group 1) spend significantly less than individuals who party four or more times (group 2). In absolute terms, they are predicted to spend 39.5 dollars less per week. This difference is statistically different from zero ($p = 0.041$). In contrast, there is no statistical difference in the spending

Table 7.7 SPSS output of a post hoc multiple comparison test

Post Hoc Tests

Multiple Comparisons

Dependent Variable: Money_Spent_Partying
Tamhane

(I) Times_Partying_1	(J) Times_Partying_1	Mean Difference (I-J)	Std. Error	Sig.	95% Confidence Interval	
					Lower Bound	Upper Bound
.00	1.00	-3.50000	7.43087	.955	-23.7758	16.7758
	2.00	-43.00000*	14.54877	.032	-82.6016	-3.3984
1.00	.00	3.50000	7.43087	.955	-16.7758	23.7758
	2.00	-39.50000*	13.30815	.041	-77.4683	-1.5317
2.00	.00	43.00000*	14.54877	.032	3.3984	82.6016
	1.00	39.50000*	13.30815	.041	1.5317	77.4683

*. The mean difference is significant at the 0.05 level.

patterns between groups 0 and 1. In absolute terms, there is a mere 3.5 dollars difference between the two groups. This difference is not statistically different from zero ($p = 0.955$).

7.2.4   Doing an *f*-Test in Stata

For our *f*-test we use money spent partying per week as the dependent variable, and as the independent variable, we use the categorical variable times partying per week. Given that we only have 40 observations and given that there should be at least several observations per category to yield valid test results, we reduce the six categories to three. In more detail, we cluster together no partying and partying once, partying twice and three times, and partying four times and five times or more. We can create this new variable by hand, or we can also have Stata do it for us. We will label this variable times partying 1.

Preliminary Procedure: Creating the variable times partying 1

Write in the Stata Command editor:

(1) generate Times_Partying_1 $= 0$
    (this creates the variable and assigns the value of 0 to all observations) (see Fig. 7.19)
(2) replace Times_Partying_1 $= 1$ if(Times_Partying ≥ 2) and Times_Partying ≤ 3
    (this assigns the value of 1 to all individuals in groups 2 and 3 for the variable times partying) (see Fig. 7.20).
(3) replace Times_Partying_1 $= 2$ if(Times_Partying ≥ 4) (see Fig. 7.21)
    (this assigns the value of 2 to all individuals in groups 4 and 5).

```
Command
generate Times_Partying_1 = 0
```

Fig. 7.19 Generating the variable Times_Partying 1 (first step)

```
Command
replace Times_Partying_1 = 2 if(Times_Partying>=4)
```

Fig. 7.20 Generating the variable Times_Partying 1 (second step)

```
Command
replace Times_Partying_1 = 2 if(Times_Partying>=4)
```

Fig. 7.21 Generating the variable Times_Partying 1 (third step)

```
Command
oneway Money_Spent_Partying Times_Partying_1, tabulate
```

Fig. 7.22 Doing an ANOVA analysis in Stata

Main analysis: conducting the ANOVA

Write in the Stata Command editor: oneway Money_Spent_Partying Times_Partying_1, tabulate (see Fig. 7.22).

7.2.5 Interpreting an *f*-Test in Stata

In the first part of the table, Stata provides summary statistics of the three group means (Table 7.8). The output reports that individuals who go out partying once a week or less spend on average 64 dollars per week. Those who party two to three times per week merely spend 3.5 dollars more than the first group. In contrast, individuals in the third group of students, who party four or more times, spend approximately 107 dollars per week partying. We also see that the standard deviations are quite large, especially for the third group—students that party four or more times per week. These descriptive statistics also give us a hint that there is probably a statistically significant difference between the third group and the two other groups. The *f*-test (Prob $> F = 0.0003$) further reveals that there are in fact differences between groups. However, the *f*-test does not allow us to detect where the differences lie. In order to gauge this, we have to conduct a multiple comparison test. However, before doing so we have to gauge whether the variances of the three

Table 7.8 Stata ANOVA output this table is misplaced here put below the text in 7.2.5

Times_Party ing_1	Summary of Money_Spent_Partying Mean	Std. Dev.	Freq.
0	64	21.186998	10
1	67.5	14.372855	20
2	107	40.838435	10
Total	76.5	30.153454	40

	Analysis of Variance				
Source	SS	df	MS	F	Prob > F
Between groups	12485	2	6242.5	10.05	0.0003
Within groups	22975	37	620.945946		
Total	35460	39	909.230769		

Bartlett's test for equal variances: chi2(2) = 14.3463   Prob>chi2 = 0.001

groups are equal or if they are dissimilar. The Bartlett's test for equal variance, which is listed below the ANOVA output, gives us this information. If the test statistic provides a statistically significant value, then we have to reject the null hypothesis of equal variances and accept the alternative hypothesis that the variances between groups are unequal. In our case, the Bartlett's test displays a statistically significant value (prob > chi2 = 0.001). Hence, we have to proceed with a post-stratification test with unequal variance.

7.2.6   Doing a Post hoc or Multiple Comparison Test with Unequal Variance in Stata

Since the Bartlett's test indicates some violation of the equal variance assumption (i.e., the distributions around the group means are different for the various groups in the sample), we have to conduct a multiple comparison test in which the unequal variance assumption is relaxed. A Stata module to compute pairwise multiple comparisons with unequal variances exists, but is not included by default and must be downloaded. To do the test we have follow a multistep procedure:

Step 1: Write in the Command field: search pwmc (see Fig. 7.23).
This brings us to a Stata page with several links—click on the first link and click on "(Click here to install)" to download the program (Once, downloaded, the program is installed and does not need to be downloaded again) (see Fig. 7.24).
Step 2: Write into the Command field: pwmc Money_Spent_Partying, over (Times_Partying_1) (Fig. 7.25).

```
Command
search pwmc
```

Fig. 7.23 Downloading a post hoc or multiple comparison test with unequal variance

```
Search of official help files, FAQs, Examples, SJs, and STBs

Web resources from Stata and other users

(contacting http://www.stata.com)

6 packages found (Stata Journal and STB listed first)
-------------------------------------------------------

pwmc from http://fmwww.bc.edu/RePEc/bocode/p
```

Fig. 7.24 Download page for the post hoc multiple comparison test

```
Command
pwmc Money_Spent_Partying, over(Times_Partying_1)
```

Fig. 7.25 Doing a post hoc or multiple comparison test with unequal variance in Stata

Stata actually provides test results of three different multiple comparison tests, all using some slightly different algebra (see Table 7.9). Regardless of the test, what we can see is that, substantively, the results of the three tests do not differ. These tests are also slightly more difficult to interpret because they do not display any significance level. Rather, we have to interpret the confidence interval to determine whether two means are statistically different from zero. We find that there is no statistically significant difference between groups 0 and 1. For example, if we look at the first of the three tests, we find that the confidence interval includes positive and negative values; it ranges from –16.90 to 23.90. Hence, we cannot accept the alternative hypothesis that groups 0 and 1 are different from one another. In contrast, we can conclude that groups 0 and 2, as well as 1 and 2, are statistically different from one another, respectively, because both confidence intervals include only positive values (i.e., the confidence interval for the difference between groups 0 and 2 ranges from 2.38 to 83.62 and the confidence interval for the difference between groups 1 and 2 ranges from 2.54 to 76.46).

Please also note that in case the Bartlett's test of equal variance (see Table 6.3) does not display any significance, a multiple comparison test assuming equal variance can be used. Stata has many options; the most prominent ones are probably the algorithms by Scheffe and Sidak. For presentation purposes, let us assume that the Bartlett test was not significant in Table 6.3.

In such a case, we would type into the Stata Command field:

Table 7.9 Stata output of post hoc multiple comparison test

Pairwise comparisons of means (unequal variances)

Money_Spent_Partying	Diff.	Std.Err	Dunnett's C [95% Conf. Interval]	
Times_Partying_1				
1 vs 0	3.5	7.43087	-16.89737	23.89737
2 vs 0	43	14.54877	2.379758	83.62024
2 vs 1	39.5	13.30815	2.538827	76.46117

Money_Spent_Partying	Diff.	Std.Err	Games and Howell [95% Conf. Interval]	
Times_Partying_1				
1 vs 0	3.5	7.43087	-16.06879	23.06879
2 vs 0	43	14.54877	4.766046	81.23395
2 vs 1	39.5	13.30815	3.095694	75.90431

Money_Spent_Partying	Diff.	Std.Err	Tamhane's T2 [95% Conf. Interval]	
Times_Partying_1				
1 vs 0	3.5	7.43087	-16.77576	23.77576
2 vs 0	43	14.54877	3.398387	82.60161
2 vs 1	39.5	13.30815	1.531734	77.46827

Command
```
oneway Money_Spent_Partying Times_Partying_1, sidak
```

Fig. 7.26 Multiple comparison test according to Sidak

oneway Money_Spent_Partying Times_Partying_1, sidak (see Fig. 7.26).

To determine whether there is a significant difference between groups, we would interpret the two-by-two table (see the second part of Table 7.10). The table highlights that the mean difference between group 0 and group 1 is 3.5 dollars, a value that is not statistically different from 0 (Sig = 0.978). In contrast the difference in spending between group 0 and group 2, which is 43 dollars, is statistically significant (sig = 0.001). The same applies to the difference in spending (39.5 dollars) between groups 1 and 2 (sig = 0.001).

Table 7.10 Multiple comparison test with equal variance in Stata

| | Analysis of Variance | | | | |
Source	SS	df	MS	F	Prob > F
Between groups	12485	2	6242.5	10.05	0.0003
Within groups	22975	37	620.945946		
Total	35460	39	909.230769		

Bartlett's test for equal variances: chi2(2) = 14.3463 Prob>chi2 = 0.001

```
                    Comparison of Money_Spen~g by Times_Part~1
                                    (Sidak)
Row Mean-|
Col Mean |         0                1

       1 |       3.5
         |     0.978

       2 |        43             39.5
         |     0.001            0.001
```

7.2.7   Reporting the Results of an *f*-Test

In Sect. 4.12, we hypothesized that individuals who party more frequently will spend more money for their weekly partying habits than individuals that party less frequently. Creating three groups of party goers—(1) students, who party once or less, on average, (2) students who party between two and three times, and (3) students who party more than four times—we find some support for our hypothesis; that is, a general *f*-test confirms (Sig = 0.0003) that there are differences between groups. Yet, the *f*-test cannot tell us between which groups the differences lie. In order to find this out, we must compute a post hoc multiple comparison test. We do so assuming unequal variances between the three distributions, because a Bartlett's test of equal variance (sig = 0.001) reveals that the null hypothesis (get rid of the plural, I cannot delete the word hypotheses) hypotheses of equal variances must be rejected. Our results indicate that the mean spending average statistically significantly differs between groups 0 and 2 [i.e., the average difference in party spending is 43 dollars (sig = 0.032)]. The same applies to the difference between groups 1 and 2 [i.e., the average difference in party spending is 39.5 dollars (Sig = 0.041)]. In contrast, there is no difference in spending between those who party once or less and those who party two or three times (sig 0.955).

7.3   Cross-tabulation Table and Chi-Square Test

7.3.1   Cross-tabulation Table

So far, we have discussed bivariate tests that work with a categorical variable as the independent variable and a continuous variable as the dependent variable (i.e., an independent samples t-test if the independent variable is binary and the dependent variable continuous and an ANOVA or f-test if the independent variable has more than two categories). What happens if both the independent and dependent variables are binary? In this case, we can present the data in a crosstab.

Table 7.11 provides an example of a two-by-two table. The table presents the results of a lab experiment with mice. A researcher has 105 mice with a severe illness; she treats 50 mice with a new drug and does not treat 55 mice at all. She wants to know whether this new drug can cure animals. To do so she creates four categories: (1) treated and dead, (2) treated and alive, (3) not treated and dead, and (4) not treated and alive.

Based on this two-by-two table, we can ask the question: How many of the dead are either treated or not treated? To answer this question, we have to use the column as unit of analysis and calculate the percentage of dead, which are treated and the percentage of dead, which are not treated. To do so, we have to convert the column raw numbers into percentages. To calculate these percentages for the first field, we take the number in the field—treated/dead—and divide it by the column total ($36/66 = 55.55\%$). We do analogously for the other fields (see Table 7.12). Interpreting Table 6.7, we can find, for example, that roughly 56% of the dead mice have been treated, but only 35.9% of those alive have undergone treatment.

Instead of asking the question how many of the dead mice have been treated, we might change the question and ask how many of the dead have been treated or alive? To get at this information, we first calculate the percentage of dead mice with treatment and of alive mice with treatment. We do analogously for the dead that are not treated and the alive that are not treated. Doing so, we find that of all treated, 72% are dead and only 28% are alive. In contrast, the not treated mice have a higher chance of survival. Only 55.55% have died and 44.45% have survived (see Table 7.13).

Table 7.11 Two-by-two table measuring the relationship between drug treatment and the survival of animals

	Dead	Alive
Treated	36	14
Not treated	30	25
Total	66	39

Table 7.12 Two-by-two table focusing on the interpretation of the columns

	Dead	Alive
Treated	36	14
Percent	55.55	35.90
Not treated	30	25
Percent	44.45	64.10
Total	66	39
Percent	100	100

Table 7.13 Two-by-two table focusing on the interpretation of the rows

	Dead	Alive	Total
Treated	36	14	50
Percent	72.00	28.00	100
Not treated	30	25	55
Total	55.55	44.45	100

Table 7.14 Calculating the expected values

	Dead	Alive	Total
Treated	36 (31.4)	14 (18.6)	50
Not treated	30 (34.6)	25 (20.4)	55
Total	66	39	105

7.3.2 Chi-Square Test

Having interpreted the crosstabs a researcher might ask whether there is a relationship between drug treatment and the survival of mice. To answer this research question, she might postulate the following hypothesis:

H_0: The survival of the animals is independent of drug treatment.
H_a: The survival of the animals is higher with drug treatment.

In order to determine if there is a relationship between drug treatment and the survival of mice, we use what is called a chi-square test. To apply this test, we compare the actual value in each field with a random distribution of values between the four fields. In other words, we compare the real value in each field with an expected value, calculated so that the chance that a mouse falls in each of the four fields is the same.

To calculate this expected value, we use the following formula:

$$\frac{\text{Row Total} \times \text{Column Total}}{\text{Table Total}}$$

Table 7.14 displays the observed and the expected values for the four possible categories: (1) treated and dead, (2) treated and alive, (3) not-treated and dead, and

(4) not-treated and alive. The logic behind a chi-square test is that the larger the gap between one or several observed and expected values, the higher the chance that there actually is a pattern or relationship in the data (i.e., that treatment has an influence on survival).

The formula for a chi-square test is:

$$X^2 = \frac{(\text{Observed} - \text{Expected})^2}{\text{Expected}}$$

In more detail the four steps to calculate a chi-square value are the following:

(1) For each observed value in the table, subtract the corresponding expected value $(O{-}E)$.
(2) Square the difference $(O{-}E)^2$.
(3) Divide the squares obtained for each cell in the table by the expected number for that cell
$(O{-}E)^2/E$.
(4) Sum all the values for $(O{-}E)^2/E$. This is the chi-square statistic.

Our treated animal example gives us a chi-square value of 3.418. This value is not high enough to reject the null hypothesis of a no effect between treatment and survival. Please note that in earlier times, researchers compared their chi-square test value with a critical value, a value that marked the 5% alpha level (i.e., a 95% degree of certainty). If their test value fell below this critical value, then the researcher could conclude that there is no difference between the groups, and if it was above, then the researcher could conclude that there is a pattern in the data. In modern times, statistical outputs display the significance level associated with a chi-square value right away, thus allowing the researcher to determine right away if there is a relationship between the two categorical variables.

A chi-square test works with the following limitations:

– No expected cell count can be less than 5.
– Larger samples are more likely to trigger statistically significant results.
– The test only identifies *that* a difference exists, not necessarily *where* it exists. (If we want to decipher where the differences are, we have look at the data and detect in what cells are the largest differences between observed and expected values. These differences are the drivers of a high chi-square value.)

7.3.3   Doing a Chi-Square Test in SPSS

The dependent variable of our study, which we used for the previous tests (i.e., t-test and f-test)—money spent partying—is continuous, and we cannot use it for our chi-square test. We have to use two categorical variables and make sure that there are

Fig. 7.27 Doing crosstabs in SPSS (first step)

least five observations in each cell. The two categorical variables we choose are gender and times partying per week. Since, we have only 40 observations, we further contract the variable times partying and create 2 categories: (1) partying a lot (three times or more a week) and partying moderately (less than 3 times a week). We name this new variable times partying 2. To create this new variable, see Sect. 7.1.2.

Step 1: Go to Analyze—Descriptive Statistics—Crosstabs (see Fig. 7.27).
Step 2: Put Gender in the Row(s) field and Times Partying 2 in the Columns field. Click on statistics (see Fig. 7.28).
Step 3: In the Crosstabs: Statistics field, check the box Chi-square—click continue— you will be redirected to the previous box—click okay (see Fig. 7.29).

7.3.4   Interpreting an SPSS Chi-Square Test

An SPSS chi-square test output consists of two parts: a cross-tabulation table and the actual chi-square test (see Table 7.15). The crosstab indicates that the sample consists of 21 guys and 19 girls. Within the 2 genders, partying habits are quite equally distributed; 9 guys party 2 times or less per week, and 12 guys party 3 times or more. For girls, the numbers are rather similar—ten girls party twice or less per week, on average, and nine girls three times or more. We already see from the chi-square table that there is hardly any difference between guys and girls. The Pearson chi-square test (i.e., first row of the chi-square test table) confirms this observation. The chi-square value is 0.382 and the corresponding significance level is 0.536, which is far above the benchmark of 0.05. Based on these test-statistics, we cannot reject the null hypothesis; this implies that we can conclude that the partying habits of guys and girls (in terms of the times per week both genders party) do not differ.

Fig. 7.28 Doing crosstabs in SPSS (second step)

Fig. 7.29 Doing crosstabs in SPSS (third step)

Table 7.15 SPSS chi-square test output

Gender * Times_Partying_2 Crosstabulation

Count

		Times_Partying_2		Total
		.00	1.00	
Gender	.00	9	10	19
	1.00	12	9	21
Total		21	19	40

Chi-Square Tests

	Value	df	Asymptotic Significance (2-sided)	Exact Sig. (2-sided)	Exact Sig. (1-sided)
Pearson Chi-Square	.382ᵃ	1	.536		
Continuity Correctionᵇ	.091	1	.763		
Likelihood Ratio	.383	1	.536		
Fisher's Exact Test				.752	.382
Linear-by-Linear Association	.373	1	.542		
N of Valid Cases	40				

a. 0 cells (0.0%) have expected count less than 5. The minimum expected count is 9.03.

b. Computed only for a 2x2 table

Fig. 7.30 Doing a chi-square test in Stata

Command

`tab Gender Times_Partying_2, chi2`

7.3.5 Doing a Chi-Square Test in Stata

To do a chi-square test, we cannot use the dependent variable of our study—money spent partying—because it is continuous. For a chi-square test to function, we have to use two categorical variables and make sure that there are at least five observations in each cell. The two categorical variables we choose are gender and times partying per week. Since we have only 40 observations, we further collapse the variable times partying and create 2 categories: (1) partying a lot (3 times or more a week) and (2) partying moderately (less than 3 times a week). We name this new variable times partying 2. To create this new variable, see Sect. 8.1.3.

Step 1: Write into the Stata Command field: tab Gender Times_Partying_2 (see Fig. 7.30)

(the order in which we write our two categorical variables does not matter).

Table 7.16 Stata chi-square output

```
tab Gender Times_Partying_2, chi2

                 Times_Partying_2
    Gender  |       0          1   |    Total
   ---------+----------------------+---------
         0  |       9         10   |      19
         1  |      12          9   |      21
   ---------+----------------------+---------
     Total  |      21         19   |      40

           Pearson chi2(1) =    0.3822   Pr = 0.536
```

The Stata test output in Table 7.16 consists of a cross-tabulation table and the actual chi-square test below. The crosstab indicates that the sample consists of 21 guys and 19 girls. Within the 2 genders, partying habits are quite equally distributed; 9 guys party 2 times or less per week, and 12 guys party 3 times or more. For girls, the numbers are rather similar: ten girls party twice or less per week, on average, and nine girls three times or more. We already see from the chi-square table that there is hardly any difference between guys and girls. The Pearson chi-square test result below the cross-table confirms this observation. The chi-square value is 0.382, and the corresponding significance level is 0.536, which is far above the benchmark of 0.05. Based on these test statistics, we can conclude that the partying habits of guys and girls (in terms of the times per week both genders party) do not differ.

7.3.6 Reporting a Chi-Square Test Result

Using a chi-square test, we have tried to detect if there is a relationship between gender and the times per week students party. We find that in absolute terms roughly about half the girls and guys, respectively, either party two times or less or three times or more. The chi-square test confirms that there is no statistically significant difference in the number of times either of two genders goes out to party (i.e., the chi-square value is 0.38 and the corresponding significance level is 0.534).

Reference

Park, H. (2009). *Comparing group means: T-tests and one-way ANOVA using Stata, SAS, R, and SPSS*. Working paper, The University Information Technology Services (UITS), Center for Statistical and Mathematical Computing, Indiana University.

Further Reading

Statistics Textbooks

Basically every introductory to statistics book covers bivariate statistics between categorical and continuous variables. The books I list here are just a short selection of possible textbooks. I have chosen these books because they are accessible and approachable and they do not use math excessively.

Brians, C. L. (2016). *Empirical political analysis: Pearson new international edition coursesmart etextbook*. London: Routledge (chapter 11). Provides a concise introduction into different types of means testing.

Macfie, B. P., & Nufrio, P. M. (2017). *Applied statistics for public policy*. New York: Routledge. This practical text provides students with the statistical tools needed to analyze data. It also shows through several examples how statistics can be used as a tool in making informed, intelligent policy decisions (part 2).

Walsh, A., & Ollenburger, J. C. (2001). *Essential statistics for the social and behavioral sciences: A conceptual approach*. Upper Saddle River: Prentice Hall (chapters 7–11). These chapters explain in rather simple forms the logic behind different types of statistical tests between categorical variables and provide real life examples.

Presenting Results in Publications

Morgan, S., Reichert, T., & Harrison, T. R. (2016). *From numbers to words: Reporting statistical results for the social sciences*. London: Routledge. This book complements introductory to statistics books. It shows scholars how they can present their test results in either visual or text form in an article or scholarly book

Bivariate Relationships Featuring Two Continuous Variables

8

Abstract

In this chapter, we discuss bivariate relationships between two continuous variables. In research, these are the relationships that occur the most often. We can express bivariate relationships between continuous variables in three ways: (1) through a graphical representation in the form of a scatterplot, (2) through a correlation analysis, and (3) through a bivariate regression analysis. We describe and explain each method and show how to implement it in SPSS and Stata.

8.1 What Is a Bivariate Relationship Between Two Continuous Variables?

A bivariate relationship involving two continuous variables can be displayed graphically and through a correlation or regression analysis. Such a relationship can exist if there is a *general* tendency for these two variables to be related, even if it is not a completely determined rule. In statistical terms, we say that these two variables "vary together"; this means that values of the variable x (the independent variable) tend to occur more often with some values of the variable y (the dependent variable) than with other values of the variable y.

8.1.1 Positive and Negative Relationships

When we describe relationships between variables, we normally distinguish between positive and negative relationships.

Positive relationship High, or above average, values of x tend to occur with high, or above average, values of y. Also, low values of x tend to occur with low values of y.

© Springer International Publishing AG 2019
D. Stockemer, *Quantitative Methods for the Social Sciences*,
https://doi.org/10.1007/978-3-319-99118-4_8

Examples:

- Income and education
- National wealth and degree of democracy
- Height and weight

Negative relationship High, or above average, values of *x* tend to occur with *low*, or *below* average, values of *y*. Also, low values of *x* tend to occur with high values of *y*.

Examples:

- State social spending and income inequality
- Exposure to Fox News and support for Democrats
- Smoking and life expectancy

8.2   Scatterplots

A scatterplot graphically describes a quantitative relationship between two continuous variables: Each dot (point) is one individual observation's value on *x* and *y*. The values of the independent variable (*X*) appear in sequence on the horizontal or *x*-axis. The values of the dependent variable (*Y*) appear on the vertical or *y*-axis. For a positive association, the points tend to move diagonally from lower left to upper right. For a negative association, the points tend to move from upper left to lower right. For NO association, points are scattered with no discernable *diagonal* line.

8.2.1   Positive Relationships Displayed in a Scatterplot

Figure 8.1 displays a positive association, or a positive relationship, between countries' per capita GDP and the amount of energy they consume. We see that even if the data do not exactly follow a line, there is nevertheless a tendency that countries with higher GDP per capita values are associated with more energy usage. In other words, higher values of the *x*-axis (the independent variable) correspond to higher values on the *y*-axis (the dependent variable).

8.2.2   Negative Relationships Displayed in a Scatterplot

Figure 8.2 displays a negative relationship between per capita GDP, and the share agriculture makes up of a country's GDP; that is, our results indicate that the richer a country becomes, the more agriculture loses its importance for the economy. In statistical terms, we find that low values of the *x*-axis correspond to high values on the *y*-axis and high values on the *x*-axis correspond to low values on the *y*-axis.

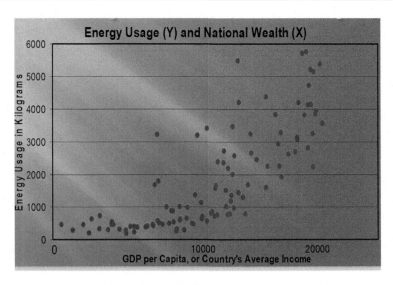

Fig. 8.1 Bivariate relationship between the GDP per capita and energy spending

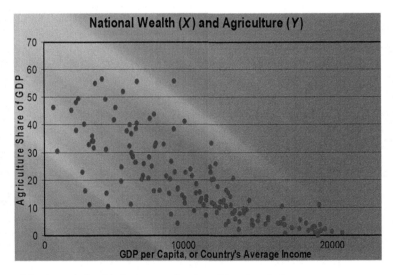

Fig. 8.2 Bivariate relationship between national wealth and agriculture

8.2.3 No Relationship Displayed in a Scatterplot

Figure 8.3 displays an instance in which the independent and dependent variable are unrelated to one another. In more detail, the graph highlights that the affluence of a country is unrelated to its size. In other words, there is no discernable direction to the points in the scatterplot.

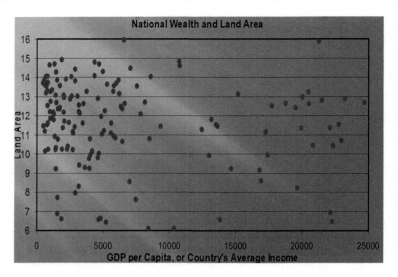

Fig. 8.3 Relationship between a country's GDP per capita and its size

8.3   Drawing the Line in a Scatterplot

The line we draw in a scatterplot is called the ordinary least square line (OLS line). In theory, we can draw a multitude of lines, but in practice we want to find the best fitting line to the data. The best fitting line is the line where the summed up distance of the points from below the line is equal to the summed up distance of the points from above the line. Figure 8.4 clearly shows a line that does not fit the data properly. The distance of all the points toward the line is much larger for the points below the line in comparison to the points above the line. In contrast, the distance of the points toward the line is the same for the points above the line as for the points below the line in Fig. 8.4. In contrast, the line in Fig. 8.5 is the best fitting line (i.e. the sum of the distance of all the points from the line is zero).

8.4   Doing Scatterplots in SPSS

For our scatterplot, we will use money spent partying as the dependent variable. For the independent variable, we will use quality of extra-curricular activities, hypothesizing that students who enjoy the university-sponsored activities will spend less money partying. Rather than going out and party, they will be in sports and social or political university clubs and partake in their activities. A scatterplot can help us confirm or disconfirm this hypothesis.

Step 1: Go to Graphs—Legacy Dialogs—Scatter/Dot (see Fig. 8.6).

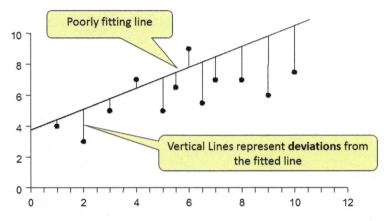

Fig. 8.4 An example of a line that fits the data poorly

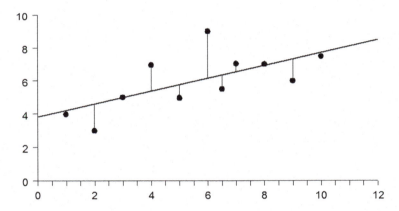

Fig. 8.5 An example of the best fitted line

Step 2: Then you see the box below—click on Simple Scatter and Define (see Fig. 8.7).

Step 3: Put the dependent variable (i.e., money spent partying) on the *y*-axis and the independent variable (quality of extra-curricular activities) on the *x*-axis. Click okay (see Fig. 8.8).

Step 4: After the completion of the steps explained in step 3, the scatterplot will show up. However, it would be nice to add a line, which can give us a more robust estimate of the relationship between the two variables. In order to include the line, double-click on the scatterplot in the output window. The chart builder below will appear. Then, just click on the line icon on the second row (the middle icon), and the scatterplot with the line will appear (see Fig. 8.9).

| File | Edit | View | Data | Transform | Analyze | Direct Marketing | Graphs | Utilities | Add-ons | Window | Help |

	Student	Money_Spent_Partying	Study_Time				Fun_Without_Alcohol	Quality_Extra_C
1	Student1	50.00	7				60.00	
2	Student2	35.00	8					
3	Student3	120.00	12	1.00	3.00	4.0		
4	Student4	80.00	3	.00	4.00	4.0		
5	Student5	100.00	11	.00	1.00	1.0		
6	Student6	120.00	14	1.00	5.00	4.0		
7	Student7	90.00	11	.00	4.00	2.0		
8	Student8	80.00	10	1.00	4.00	3.0		
9	Student9	70.00	9	.00	3.00	3.0		
10	Student10	80.00	8	1.00	2.00	3.0		
11	Student11	60.00	12	1.00	4.00	2.0		
12	Student12	50.00	14	1.00	2.00	1.0		
13	Student13	100.00	13	.00	3.00	4.0		
14	Student14	90.00	15	.00	3.00			

Menu options shown: Chart Builder..., Graphboard Template Chooser..., Weibull Plot..., Compare Subgroups, Regression Variable Plots, Legacy Dialogs — Bar..., 3-D Bar..., Line..., Area..., Pie..., High-Low..., Boxplot..., Error Bar..., Population Pyramid..., Scatter/Dot..., Histogram...

Fig. 8.6 Doing a scatterplot in SPSS (first step)

Fig. 8.7 Doing a scatterplot in SPSS (second step)

As expected, Fig. 8.9 displays a negative relationship between the quality of extra-curricular activities and the money students spent partying. The graph displays that students who think that the extra-curricular activities offered by the university are poor do in fact spend more money per week partying. In contrast, students who like the sports and social and political clubs at their university are less likely to spend a lot of money partying. Because we can see that the line is relatively steep, we can already detect that the relationship is relatively strong; a bivariate regression analysis (see below) will give us some information about the strength of this relationship.

Fig. 8.8 Doing a scatterplot in SPSS (third step)

8.5   Doing Scatterplots in Stata

For our scatterplot, we will use money spent partying as the dependent variable. For the independent variable, we will use quality of extra-curricular activities, hypothesizing that students who enjoy the university-sponsored free time activities will spend less money partying. Rather than going out and party, they will be involved in sports or social and political university clubs and partake in their activities. A scatterplot can help us confirm or disconfirm this hypothesis.

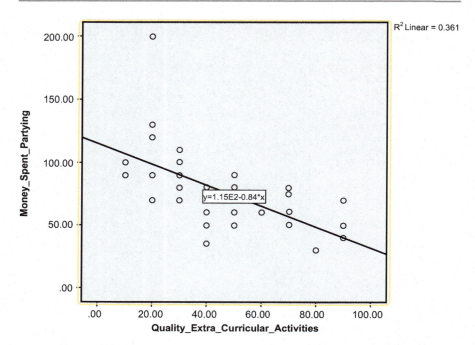

Fig. 8.9 SPSS scatterplot between the quality of extra-curricular activities and money spent partying per week

Step 1: Type in the command editor:
graph twoway (scatter Money_Spent_Partying Quality_Extra_Curricular_Activ) (lfit Money_Spent_Partying Quality_Extra_Curricular_Activ)[1] (see Fig. 8.10).

Figure 8.11 displays a negative slope, that is, the graph displays that students who think that the extra-curricular activities offered by the university are poor do in fact spend more money partying. In contrast, students who like the sports, social, and political clubs at their university are less likely to spend a lot of money partying. Because we can see that the line is relatively steep, we can already detect that the relationship is relatively strong; a bivariate regression analysis (see below) will give us some information about the strength of this relationship.

Command
graph twoway (scatter Money_Spent_Partying Quality_Extra_Curricular_Activities)(lfit Money_Spent_Partying Quality_Extra_Curricular_Activities)

Fig. 8.10 Doing a scatterplot in Stata

---

[1] In the dataset, you might want to write Atktiv because writing out activities makes the word too long to fit into the data field in Stata.

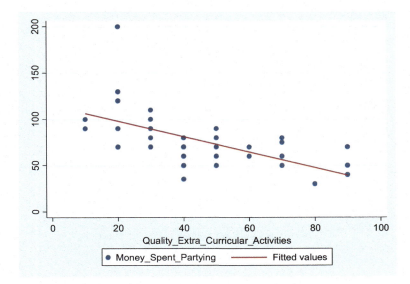

Fig. 8.11 Stata scatterplot between the quality of extra-curricular activities and the money spent partying

Step 2: Stata allows us to include the confidence interval around the fitted line:
graph twoway (scatter Money_Spent_Partying Quality_Extra_Curricular_Activ) (lfitci Money_Spent_Partying Quality_Extra_Curricular_Activ) (see Fig. 8.12).

Assuming that our sample was randomly picked from a population of university students, the confidence interval in Fig. 8.13 depicts the range around the fitted line in which the real relationship falls. In other words, the population line displaying the relationship between the independent and dependent variable should be anywhere in the gray shaded area.

```
Command
graph twoway (scatter Money_Spent_Partying Quality_Extra_Curricular_Activities)(lfitci Money_Spent_Partying Quality_Extra_Curricular_Activities)
```

Fig. 8.12 Doing a scatterplot with confidence interval in Stata

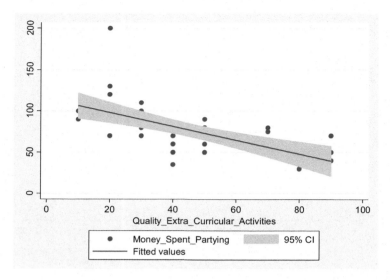

Fig. 8.13 Stata scatterplot between the quality of extra-curricular activities and the money spent partying with the confidence interval

8.6 Correlation Analysis

A correlation analysis is closely linked to the analysis of scatterplots. In order to do a correlation analysis, the relationship between independent and dependent variable must be linear. In other words, we must be able to use a line to express the relationship between the independent variable x and the dependent variable y. To interpret a scatterplot, two things are important: (1) the direction of the line (i.e., a relationship can only exist if the fitted line is either positive or negative) and (2) the closeness of the points toward the line (i.e., the closer the points are clustered around the line, the stronger the correlation is). In fact, in a correlation analysis, it is solely the second point, the closeness of the points to the line that helps us determine the strength of the relationship. To highlight, if we move from graph 1 to graph 4 in Fig. 8.14, we can see that the points get closer to the line for each of the fourth graphs. Hence, the correlation between the two variables becomes stronger.

In statistical terms, the correlation coefficient, also called Pearson correlation coefficient, is denoted by r. It expresses both the *strength* and *direction* of a relationship between two variables in a single number. If the dots line up to exactly one line, we have a perfect correlation or a correlation coefficient of 1. In contrast, the more all over the place the dots are, the more the correlation coefficient approaches 0 (see Fig. 8.3). In terms of direction, a correlation coefficient with a positive sign depicts a positive correlation, whereas a correlation coefficient with a negative sign depicts a negative correlation.

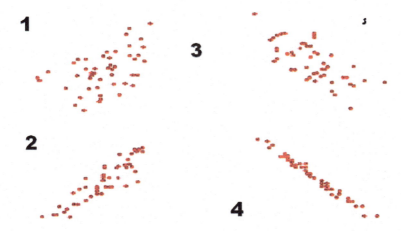

Fig. 8.14 Assessing the strength of relationships in correlation analysis

Formula for r:

$$r = \frac{1}{n-1} \sum_{i=1}^{n} \left(\frac{x_i - \bar{x}}{S_x} \right) \left(\frac{y_i - \bar{y}}{S_y} \right)$$

Properties of r:

– $-1 < r < 1$.
– $r > 0$ means a positive relationship—the stronger the relationship, the closer r is to 1.
– $r < 0$ means a negative relationship—the stronger the relationship, the closer r is to -1.
– $r = 0$ means no relationship.

Benchmarks for establishing the level of correlation:

$(-) 0.3 < r < (-) 0.45 =$ weak correlation
$(-) 0.45 < r < (-) 0.6 =$ medium strong correlation
$r < (-) 0.6 =$ strong correlation

R, like the mean and the standard deviation, is sensitive to outliers. For example, Fig. 8.15 displays nearly identical scatterplots, with the sole difference being that we add an outlier to graph 2. Adding this outlier decreases the correlation coefficient by 0.2 points. Given that the line is drawn so that the sum of the points below the line and the sum of the points above the line equal 0, an outlier pushes the line in one direction (in our case downward), thus increasing the distance of each point toward the line, which, in turn, decreases the strength of the correlation.

Fig. 8.15 *R* with and without an outlier

There are two important caveats with correlation analysis. First, since a correlation analysis defines strength at how close the points in a scatterplot are toward a line, it does not provide us with any indication of the strength in impact, in the substantial sense, of a relationship of an independent on a dependent variable. Second, a correlation analysis depicts only whether two variables are related and how closely they follow a positive or a negative direction. It does not give us any indication which variable is the cause and which is the effect.

8.6.1 Doing a Correlation Analysis in SPSS

Step 1: Go to Analyze—Correlate—Bivariate (see Fig. 8.16).

Fig. 8.16 Doing a correlation in SPSS (first step)

Fig. 8.17 Doing a correlation in SPSS (second step)

Step 2: Choose the continuous variables you want to correlate and click okay (see Fig. 8.17).

It is important to note the correlation analysis only functions with continuous variables. We have five continuous variables in our data and will include them all in the correlation matrix. These five variables are (1) money spent partying, (2) quality of extra-curricular activities, (3) the amount of tuition students pay themselves, (4) whether or not students can have fun without alcohol when they go out, and (5) their study time per week.

8.6.2 Interpreting an SPSS Correlation Output

The correlation output in Table 8.1 displays the bivariate correlations between the five continuous variables in our dataset. To determine whether two variables are correlated, we first look at the significance or alpha level for each correlation. If we find that sig >0.05, we can conclude that the two variables are not correlated. In this case, we do not interpret the correlation coefficient, which should be small anyways. If we find a significant p-value (sig, ≤ 0.05), we can go on and interpret the strength of the correlation using the benchmarks provided in Sect. 8.6. To highlight, let us

Table 8.1 SPSS correlation output

Correlations

		Quality_Extra _Curricular_A ctivities	Amount_Tuiti on_Student_ Pays	Money_Spent _Partying	Fun_Without_ Alcohol	Study_Time
Quality_Extra_Curricular_ Activities	Pearson Correlation	1	-.090	-.600**	.062	-.133
	Sig. (2-tailed)		.580	.000	.706	.414
	N	40	40	40	40	40
Amount_Tuition_Student _Pays	Pearson Correlation	-.090	1	.247	.010	-.195
	Sig. (2-tailed)	.580		.125	.953	.228
	N	40	40	40	40	40
Money_Spent_Partying	Pearson Correlation	-.600**	.247	1	-.206	.171
	Sig. (2-tailed)	.000	.125		.201	.291
	N	40	40	40	40	40
Fun_Without_Alcohol	Pearson Correlation	.062	.010	-.206	1	-.777**
	Sig. (2-tailed)	.706	.953	.201		.000
	N	40	40	40	40	40
Study_Time	Pearson Correlation	-.133	-.195	.171	-.777**	1
	Sig. (2-tailed)	.414	.228	.291	.000	
	N	40	40	40	40	40

**. Correlation is significant at the 0.01 level (2-tailed).

look at the correlation between the amount of tuition students pay and the amount of time students generally dedicate to their studies per week; we find that there is no correlation between these two variables. The significance or alpha level (denoted p in statistical language) is 0.228, which is much higher than the benchmark of 0.05. Hence, we would conclude from there that there is no relationship between these two variables. In other words, we would stop our interpretation here, and we would not interpret the correlation coefficient, because it is not statistically significant. In contrast, if we look at the relationship between the variable money spent partying and the variable quality of extra-curricular activities, we find that the significance level is 0.000. This means that we can be nearly 100% sure that there is a correlation between the two variables. Having established that a correlation exists, we can now look at the sign and the magnitude of the coefficient. We find that the sign is negative, indicating that the more money students spend while going out, the less they participate in extra-curricular activities in their university. Knowing that there is a negative correlation, we can now interpret the magnitude of the correlation coefficient, which is −0.600, indicating that we have medium strong to strong negative correlation. In addition to the correlation between the quality of extra-curricular activities and money spent partying, there is one more statistically significant and substantively strong correlation, namely, between students' study time per week and whether or not they can have fun partying without alcohol. This correlation is significant at the 0.000 level and substantively strong (i.e., $r = -0.777$). The negative sign further highlights that it is negative indicating that high values for one variable trigger low values for the other variables. In this case, this implies that students that study a lot also think that they can have a lot of fun without alcohol when they party.

8.6.3 Doing a Correlation Analysis in Stata

It is important to note that correlation analyses only function with continuous variables. We have five continuous variables in our data and include them in the Stata correlation matrix: (1) money spent partying, (2) quality of extra-curricular activities, (3) the amount of tuition students pay themselves, (4) whether or not students can have fun without alcohol when they go out, and (5) their study time per week.

Step 1: Write in the command editor

pwcorr Money_Spent_Partying Study_Time Fun_Without_Alcohol Quality_Extra_Curricular_Activ Amount_Tuition_Student_Pays, sig (see Fig. 8.18)

The correlation output in Table 8.2 displays the bivariate correlations between the five continuous variables in our dataset. For each bivariate correlation, Stata provides the Pearson correlation coefficient and the significance level (p). For example, 0.1711 is the correlation coefficient between study time and money spent partying. The second number (0.29) is the corresponding significance level. To determine whether two variables are correlated, we first look at the significance or alpha level for each correlation. If we find that sig >0.05, we can conclude that the two variables are not correlated. In this case, we do not interpret the correlation coefficient, which should be small anyways. In cases where we find a significant p-value (sig <0.05), we can go on and interpret the strength of the correlation using the benchmarks provided in Sect. 8.6. To highlight, let us look at the correlation between

Command

pwcorr Money_Spent_Partying Study_Time Fun_Without_Alcohol Quality_Extra_Curricular_Activ Amount_Tuition_Student_Pays, sig

Fig. 8.18 Doing a correlation in Stata

Table 8.2 Stata correlation output

	Money_~g	Study_~e	Fun_Wi~1	Qualit~v	Amount~s
Money_Spen~g	1.0000				
Study_Time	0.1711 0.2912	1.0000			
Fun_Withou~l	-0.2064 0.2012	-0.7774 0.0000	1.0000		
Quality_Ex~v	-0.6005 0.0000	-0.1329 0.4136	0.0616 0.7057	1.0000	
Amount_Tui~s	0.2468 0.1247	-0.1950 0.2279	0.0096 0.9533	-0.0901 0.5802	1.0000

the amount of tuition students pay and the amount of time students generally dedicate to their studies per week; we find that there is no correlation between these two variables. The significance or alpha level (denoted p in statistical language) is 0.228, which is much higher than the benchmark of 0.05. Hence, we would conclude from there that there is no correlation between these two variables. In other words, we would stop our interpretation here, and we would not interpret the correlation coefficient, because it is not statistically different from zero. In contrast, if we look at the relationship between the variable money spent partying and the variable quality of extra-curricular activities, we find that the significance level is 0.000. This means that we can be nearly 100% sure that there is a correlation between the two variables. Having established that a correlation exists, we can now look at the sign and the magnitude of the coefficient. We find that the sign is negative, indicating that the more students spend money while going out, the less they participate in extra-curricular activities in their university. Knowing that there is a negative correlation, we can now interpret the magnitude of the correlation coefficient, which is −0.601, indicating that we have a medium strong to strong negative correlation. In addition to the correlation between the quality of extra-curricular activities and money spent partying, there is one more statistically significant and substantively strong correlation, namely, between students' study time per week and whether or not they can have fun partying without alcohol. This correlation is significant at the 0.000 level and substantively strong (i.e., $r = -0.762$). The negative sign further highlights that it is a negative relationship, indicating that high values for one variable trigger low values for the other variables. In this case, this implies that students that study a lot also think that they can have a lot of fun without alcohol when they party.

8.7   Bivariate Regression Analysis

In correlation analyses, we look at the direction of the line (positive or negative) and at how closely the points of the scatterplot follow that line. This allows us to detect the degree to which two variables covary, but it does not allow us to determine how strongly an independent variable influences a dependent variable. In regression analysis, we are interested in the magnitude of the influence of independent on dependent variable, as measured by the steepness of the slope. To determine the influence of an independent variable on a dependent variable, two things are important: (1) the steeper the slope, the more strongly the independent variable impacts the dependent variable. (2) The closer the points are to the line, the more certain we can be that this relationship actually exists.

8.7.1   Gauging the Steepness of a Regression Line

To explain the notion that a steeper slope indicates a stronger relationship, let us compare the two graphs in Fig. 8.19. Both graphs depict a perfect relationship, meaning that all the points are on a straight line. The correlation for both would be 1. However, we can see that the first line is much steeper than the second line.

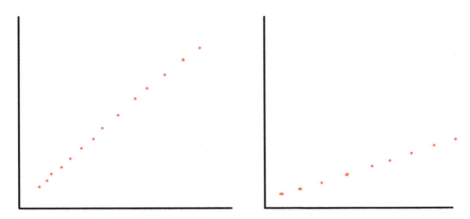

Fig. 8.19 Two regression lines featuring a strong and weak relationship, respectively

In other words, the *y* value grows stronger with higher *x* values. In contrast, the second line only moves slightly upward. Consequently, the regression coefficient is higher in the first compared to the second graph.

To determine the relationship between *x* and *y*, we use a point slope:

$$y = a + bx$$

y is the dependent variable.
x is the independent variable.
b is the slope of the line.
a is the intercept (*y* when $x = 0$).

The formula for the regression line:

$$b = r\frac{S_y}{S_x} \qquad a = \bar{y} - b\bar{x}$$

When we draw the regression line, we could in theory draw an infinite number of lines. The line that explains the data best is the line that has the smallest sum of squared errors. In statistical terms, this line is called the least square line (OLS line).

Figure 8.20 displays the least square line between the independent variable average GDP per capita per country and the dependent variable energy usage in kilograms of oil per person. The equation denoting this relationship is as follows: energy usage = 318 + 0.25 average country GDP per capita.

This means 318 kg is the amount of energy that an average citizen uses when GDP is at 0. The equation further predicts that for every 1 unit (dollar) increase on the *y*-axis, *y* values increase by 0.25 kg. So in this example, this means that for each extra dollar the average citizen in a country becomes richer, she uses 0.25 kg more of energy (oil) per year. To render the interpretation more tangible, the equation would

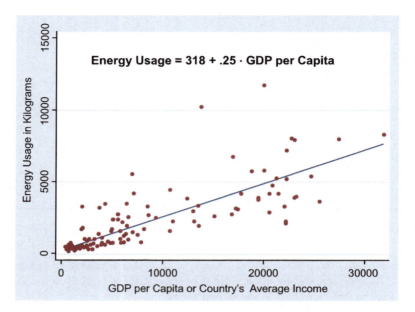

Fig. 8.20   The equation between per capita GDP and energy usage

predict that a resident in a country, where the average citizens earn 10,000 dollars, is predicted to consume 2818 kg of energy (318 + 0.25 × 10000 = 2818).

8.7.2   Gauging the Error Term

The metric we use to determine the magnitude of a relationship between an independent and a dependent variable is the steepness of the slope. As a rule, we can say that the steeper the slope, the more certain we can be that a relationship exists. However, the steepness of the slope is not the only criterion we use to determine whether or not an independent variable relates to a dependent variable. Rather, we also have to look how close the data points are to the line. The closer the points are to the line, the less error there is in the data. Figure 8.21 displays two identical lines measuring the relationship between age in months and height in centimeters for babies and toddlers. What we can see is that the relationship is equally strong for the two lines. However, the data fits the first line much better than the second line. There is more "noise" in the data in the second line, thus rendering the estimation of each of the points or observations less exact in the second line compared to the first line.

Figure 8.22 graphically explains what we mean by error term or residual. The error term or residual in a regression analysis measures the distance from each data point to the regression line. The farther any single observation or data point is away from the line, the less this observation fits the general relationship. The larger the average distance is from the line, the less well does the average data point fits the linear prediction. In other words, the greater the distance between the average data

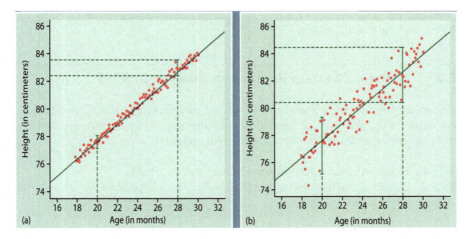

Fig. 8.21 Better and worse fitting data

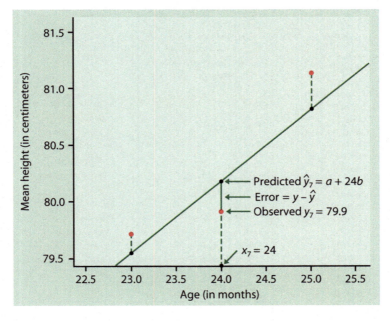

Fig. 8.22 The error term in a regression analysis

point and the line, the less we can be assured that the relationship portrayed by the regression line actually exists.

8.8   Doing a Bivariate Regression Analysis in SPSS

To conduct the bivariate regression analysis, we take the same variables we used for the scatterplots, that is, our dependent variable money spent partying and the independent variable quality of extra-curricular activities

Step 1: Go to—Analyze—Regression—Linear (see Fig. 8.23).
Step 2: Choose the dependent variable—choose the independent variable—click okay (Fig. 8.24).

Fig. 8.23 Doing a regression analysis in SPSS (first step)

Fig. 8.24 Doing a regression analysis in SPSS (second step)

8.9   Interpreting an SPSS (Bivariate) Regression Output

The SPSS regression output consists of three tables: (1) a model summary table, (2) an ANOVA output, and (3) a coefficients' table. We interpret each table separately

8.9.1   The Model Summary Table

The model summary table (see Table 8.3) indicates how well the model fits the data. It consists of four parameters: (1) the Pearson correlation coefficient (r), (2) the R-squared value, (3) the adjusted R-squared value, and (4) the standard error of the estimate.

Table 8.3 SPSS model summary table

Model Summary				
Model	R	R Square	Adjusted R Square	Std. Error of the Estimate
1	.600[a]	.361	.344	24.42734
a. Predictors: (Constant), Quality_Extra_Curricular_Activities				

R is the correlation coefficient between the real data points and the values predicted by the model. For the example at hand, the correlation coefficient is high indicating that real values and predicated values correlate at the level of 0.600.

R-squared is the most important parameter in the model summary statistic's table and is a measure of model fit (i.e., it is the squared correlation between the model's predicted values and the real values). It explains how much of the variance in the dependent variable the independent variable(s) in the model explain. In theory, the *R*-squared values can range from 0 to 1. An *R*-squared value of 0 means that the independent variable(s) do not explain any of the variance of the dependent variable, and a value of 1 signifies that the independent variable(s) explain all the variance in the dependent variable. In our example, the *R*-squared value of 0.361 implies that the independent variable—the quality of extra-curricular activities—explains 36.1% of the variance in the dependent variable, the money students spent partying per week.

The adjusted *R*-squared is a second statistic of model fit. It helps us compare different models. In real research, it might be helpful to compare models with a different number of independent variables to determine which of the alternative models is superior in a statistical sense. To highlight, the *R*-squared will always increase or remain constant if I add variables. Yet, a new variable might not add anything substantial to the model. Rather, some of the increase in *R*-squared could be simply due to coincidental variation in a specific sample. Therefore, the adjusted *R*-squared will be smaller than the *R*-squared since it controls for some of the idiosyncratic variance in the original estimate. As such, the adjusted *R*-squared is a measure of model fit adjusted for the number of independent variables in the model. It helps us compare different models; the best fitting model is always the model with the highest adjusted *R*-squared (not the model with the highest *R*-squared).[2] In our sample, the adjusted *R*-squared is 0.344 (We do not interpret this estimator in bivariate regression analysis).

The standard error of the estimate is the standard deviation of the error term and the square root of the mean square residual (or error). (Normally, we do not interpret this estimator when we conduct regression models.) In our sample, the standard error of the estimate is 24.43.

8.9.2   The Regression ANOVA Table

The *f*-test in a regression model works like an *f*-test or ANOVA analysis (see Table 8.4). It is an indication of the significance of the model (does the regression equation fit the observed data adequately?). If the *f*-ratio is significant, the regression equation has predictive power, which means that we have at least one statistically significant variable in the model. In contrast, if the *f*-test is not significant, then none of the variables in the model is statistically significant, and the model has no predictive power. In our sample, the *f*-value is 21.43, and the corresponding significance level is 0.000. Hence, we can already conclude that our independent

---

[2]Please note that we can only compare adjusted *R*-squared values of different models, if these models have the same number of observations.

Table 8.4 SPSS ANOVA table of the regression output

ANOVA[a]

Model		Sum of Squares	df	Mean Square	F	Sig.
1	Regression	12785.588	1	12785.588	21.427	.000[b]
	Residual	22674.412	38	596.695		
	Total	35460.000	39			

a. Dependent Variable: Money_Spent_Partying

b. Predictors: (Constant), Quality_Extra_Curricular_Activities

variable—the quality of extra-curricular activities—influences our dependent variable, the money students spend per week partying.

8.9.3 The Regression Coefficient Table

The coefficients' table (see Table 8.5) is the most important part of a regression output. It tells us how the independent variable relates to the dependent variable. A coefficients' table has the following statistics:

Unstandardized Regression Weights The first column portrays the unstandardized regression weights, which give us an indication of how the independent variable (s) relates to the dependent variable. In our example, the unstandardized regression weight or coefficient depicting the influence of extra-curricular activities on students' party spending is –0.839. The constant is 114.87. In other words, the –0.839 is the slope coefficient; it indicates the change in the DV associated with a 1-unit change in the IV. In our example, this implies that for each point on the 0–100 scale, students like the extra-curricular activities more, their party spending decreases by 0.839 dollars per week. The 114.87 is the predicted spending pattern if the independent

Table 8.5 The SPSS regression coefficients'.

Coefficients[a]

Model		Unstandardized Coefficients		Standardized Coefficients	t	Sig.
		B	Std. Error	Beta		
1	(Constant)	114.869	9.145		12.561	.000
	Quality_Extra_Curricular_Activities	-.839	.181	-.600	-4.629	.000

a. Dependent Variable: Money_Spent_Partying

variable has the value 0 (i.e., if students think that the extra-curricular activities at their university are very bad).

We can also express this relationship in a regression equation: $y = 114.87 - 0.839x$.

The Standard Error This statistic gives us an indication of how much variation there is around the predicted coefficient. As a rule, we can say that the smaller the standard error in relation to the regression weight is, the more certainty we can have in the interpretation of our relationship. In our case, the standard error behind the relationship between extra-curricular activities and money spent partying is 0.181.

Standardized Regression Coefficients (Beta) In multiple regression models, it is impossible to compare the magnitude of the coefficients of the independent variables. To highlight, the variable gender is a dummy variable coded 0 for guys and 1 for girls. In contrast, the variable fun without alcohol is a variable coded on a 100-point scale (i.e., 0–100). Unstandardized weights are standardized coefficients that allow us to compare the effect size of several independent variables. To do so, SPSS converts the unstandardized coefficients to z-scores (i.e., weights with mean of zero and standard deviation of 1.0). The size of the standardized regression weights gives us some indication of the importance of the variable in the regression equation. In a multiple regression analysis, it allows us to determine the relative strength of each independent variable in comparison to other variables on the dependent variable. The standardized beta is –0.600 in our bivariate model.

T-value The t-test compares the unstandardized regression against a predicted value of zero (i.e., no contribution to regression equation). It does so by dividing the unstandardized regression coefficient (i.e., our measure of effect size) by the standard error (i.e., our measure of variability in the data). As a rule, we can say that the higher the T-value, the higher the chance that we have a statistically significant relationship (see significance value). In our example, the T-value is –4.629 (–0.839/ 0.181).

Significance Value (Alpha Level) The significance level (sig) indicates the probability that a specific independent variable impacts the dependent variable. In our example, the significance level is 0.000, which implies that we can be nearly 100% sure that the quality of extra-curricular activities influences students' spending patterns while partying.

8.10   Doing a (Bivariate) Regression Analysis in Stata

To conduct the regression analysis, we will use the same variables that we used for the scatterplots, that is, our dependent variable is money spent partying and our independent variable is the quality of extra-curricular activities (see Table 7.11).

Command
reg Money_Spent_Partying Quality_Extra_Curricular_Activ

Fig. 8.25 Doing a bivariate regression analysis in Stata

Step 1: Write into the command editor: reg Money_Spent_Partying Quality_Extra_Curricular_Activ (see Fig. 8.25).

8.10.1 Interpreting a Stata (Bivariate) Regression Output

On the following pages, we explain how to interpret a Stata bivariate regression output (see Table 8.6):

Number of obs   indicates how many observations the model is based upon

The *f*-test provides the *f*-test value for the regression analysis. It works like an *f*-test or ANOVA analysis and gives an indication of the significance of the model (i.e., it measures whether the regression equation fits the observed data adequately). If the *f*-ratio is significant, the regression equation has predictive power, which means that we have at least one statistically significant variable in the model. In contrast, if the *f*-test is not significant, then none of the variables in the model is statistically significant, and the model has no predictive power. In our sample, the *f*-value is 21.43 and the corresponding significance level is 0.000 (Prob > F). Hence, we can already conclude that our independent variable—the quality of extra-curricular activities—influences our dependent variable, the money students spend per week partying. (The Table you see to the left of the summary statistics (i.e., Number of obs, *F*, Prob > F, R-squared, Adj R-squared, Root MSE) is the summary statistics of the *f*-test (see section on *t*-test or ANOVA for more details).)

Table 8.6 The Stata bivariate regression

Source	SS	df	MS				Number of obs	=	40
							F(1, 38)	=	21.43
Model	12785.588	1	12785.588				Prob > F	=	0.0000
Residual	22674.412	38	596.695054				R-squared	=	0.3606
							Adj R-squared	=	0.3437
Total	35460	39	909.230769				Root MSE	=	24.427

Money_Spent_Partying	Coef.	Std. Err.	t	P>|t|	[95% Conf. Interval]	
Quality_Extra_Curricular_Activ	-.8386742	.1811795	-4.63	0.000	-1.205453	-.471895
_cons	114.8693	9.144632	12.56	0.000	96.357	133.381

R-squared is an important parameter when we interpret a regression output. It is a measure of model fit (i.e., it is the squared correlation between the model's predicted values and the real values). It explains how much of the variation in the dependent variable is explained by the independent variables in the model. In theory, the *R*-squared values can range from 0 to 1. An *R*-squared value of 0 means that the independent variable(s) do not explain anything in the variance of the dependent variable. An *R*-squared value of 1 signifies that the independent variable(s) explain all the variance in the dependent variable. In our example, the *R*-squared value of 0.361 implies that the independent variable—the quality of extra-curricular activities— explains 36.1% of the variance in the dependent variable, the money students spent partying per week.

The adjusted *R*-squared is a second statistic of model fit that helps us compare different models. In real research, it might be helpful to compare models with a different number of independent variables to determine which of the alternative models is superior in a statistical sense. To highlight, the *R*-squared will always increase or remain constant if I add variables even though a new variable might not add anything substantial to the model. Rather, some of the increase in the *R*-squared could be simply due to coincidental variation in a specific sample. Therefore, the adjusted *R*-squared will be smaller than the *R*-squared since it controls for some of the idiosyncratic variance in the original estimate. Therefore, the adjusted *R* is a measure of model fit adjusted for the number of independent variables in the model. It helps us to compare different models; the best fitting model is always the model with the highest adjusted *R*-squared (not the model with the highest *R*-squared).[3] In our sample, the adjusted *R*-squared is 0.344. (We do not interpret this estimator in bivariate regression analysis.)

The root MSE (root mean squared error) is the standard deviation of the error term and the square root of the mean square residual (or error). (Normally, we do not interpret this estimator when we conduct regression models.) In our sample, the standard error of the estimate is 24.43.

Coef. (coefficient) The first column portrays the unstandardized regression weights, which give us an indication of how the independent variable(s) relate to the dependent variable. In our example, the unstandardized regression weight or coefficient depicting the influence of extra-curricular activities on students' party spending is—0.839. The constant is 114.87. In other words, the –0.839 is the slope coefficient; it indicates the change in the dependent variable associated with a 1-unit change in the independent variable. In our example, this implies that for each additional point on the 0–100 scale that students like the extra-curricular activities, their party spending decreases by 0.839 dollars per week. The constant (cons) coefficient of 114.87 is the predicted spending pattern if the independent variable

---

[3]Ibid.

has the value 0 (i.e., this implies that if students do not like the extra-curricular activities at their school at all, they are predicted to spend 115 dollars per week partying).

We can also express this relationship in a regression equation: $y = 114.87 - 0.839x$

The standard error gives us an indication of how much variation there is around the predicted coefficient. As a rule, we can say that the smaller the standard error relative to the regression weight, the more certainty we can have in the interpretation of our relationship between independent and dependent variable. In our case, the standard error behind the relationship between extra-curricular activities and money spent partying is 0.181.

Standardized regression coefficients (beta) In multiple regression models, it is impossible to compare the magnitude of the coefficients of the independent variables. To highlight, the variable gender is a dummy variable coded 0 for guys and 1 for girls. In contrast, the variable fun without alcohol is a variable coded on a 100-point scale (i.e., 0–100). Standardized weights are standardized coefficients that allow us to compare the effect size of several independent variables. To do so, Stata converts the unstandardized coefficients to z-scores (i.e., weights with mean of zero and standard deviation of 1). The size of the standardized regression weights gives us some indication of the importance of the variable in the regression equation. In a multiple regression analysis, it allows us to determine the relative strength of each independent variable in comparison to other variables on the dependent variable. The standardized beta is not one of the default options in the Stata package. However, it can be easily calculated. To do so, add the option beta at the end of the regression analysis. Put in the command field:

reg Money_Spent_Partying Quality_Extra_Curricular_Activ, beta (see Fig. 8.26)

In our bivariate example, the standardized beta coefficient is –0.600 (see Table 8.7).

_T_-value The _t_-test compares the unstandardized regression weight against a predicted value of zero (i.e., no contribution to regression equation). It does so by dividing the unstandardized regression coefficient (i.e., our measure of effect size) by the standard error (i.e., our measure of variability in the data). As a rule, we can say that the higher the _t_-value, the higher the chance that we have a statistically significant relationship (see significance value). In our example, the _t_-value is –4.629 (–0.839/0.181).

```
Command
reg Money_Spent_Partying Quality_Extra_Curricular_Activities, beta
```

Fig. 8.26 Doing a bivariate regression analysis with standardized beta coefficients

Table 8.7 The Stata bivariate regression table with standardized coefficients

Source	SS	df	MS			
				Number of obs	=	40
				F(1, 38)	=	21.43
Model	12785.588	1	12785.588	Prob > F	=	0.0000
Residual	22674.412	38	596.695054	R-squared	=	0.3606
				Adj R-squared	=	0.3437
Total	35460	39	909.230769	Root MSE	=	24.427

Money_Spent_Partying	Coef.	Std. Err.	t	P>|t|	Beta
Quality_Extra_Curricular_Activ	-.8386742	.1811795	-4.63	0.000	-.6004695
_cons	114.8693	9.144632	12.56	0.000	.

***P* > *t* is the significance value or alpha level** The significance level determines the probability with which we can determine that a specific independent variable impacts the dependent variable. In our example, the significance level is 0.000, which implies that we can be nearly 100% sure that the quality of extra-curricular activities influences students' spending patterns while partying.

(95% conf. interval) Assuming that our sample was randomly picked from a population of university students, the confidence interval depicts the interval in which the real relationship between the perceived quality of extra-curricular activities and students spending patterns lies. Our coefficient for the quality of extra-curricular activities has a confidence interval that ranges from –1.21 to –0.472. This means that the relationship in the population could be anywhere in this range. Similarly, the confidence interval around the constant implies that somebody who rates the quality of extra-curricular activities at 0 is expected to spend between 96.36 dollars and 133.38 for partying in a week.

8.10.2 Reporting and Interpreting the Results of a Bivariate Regression Model

When we report the results of bivariate regression model, we report the coefficient, standard error, and significance level, as well as the R-squared and the number of observations in the model. In an article or report, we would report the results as follows: Table 8.8 reports the results of a bivariate regression model measuring the influence of the quality of extra-curricular activities on students' weekly spending patterns when they party based on a survey conducted with 40 undergraduate students at a Canadian university. The model portrays a negative and statistically significant relationship between the two variables. In substantive terms, the model predicts that for every point students' evaluation of the extra-curricular activities at their university increases, they spent 84 cents less per week partying. This influence is substantial. For example, somebody, who thinks that the extra-curricular activities at her university are poor (and rates them at 20), is predicted to spend approximately 98 dollars for party activities. In contrast, somebody, who likes the extra-curricular

Table 8.8 Reporting a bivariate regression outcome

	Coefficient	Std. error	Sig
Quality of extra-curricular activities	−0.839	0.181	0.000
Constant	114.87	9.14	0.000
R-squared	0.34		
N	40		

activities (and rates them at 80), is only expected to 48 dollars for her weekly partying. The R-squared of the model further highlights that the independent variable, the quality of extra-curricular activities, explains 34% of the variance in the dependent variable partying spending per week.

Further Reading

Gravetter, F. J., & Forzano, L. A. B. (2018). *Research methods for the behavioral sciences*. Boston: Cengage Learning (chapter 12). Nice introduction into correlational research; covers the data and methods for correlational analysis, applications of the correlational strategy, and strength and weakness of the correlational research strategy.

Montgomery, D. C., Peck, E. A., & Vining, G. G. (2012). *Introduction to linear regression analysis* (Vol. 821). San Francisco: John Wiley & Sons (chapters 1 and 2). Chapters 1 and 2 provide a hands on and practical introduction into linear regression modelling, first in the bivariate realm and then in the multivariate realm.

Ott, R. L., & Longnecker, M. T. (2015). *An introduction to statistical methods and data analysis*. Toronto, ON: Nelson Education (chapter 11). Provides a good introduction into correlation and regression analysis clearly highlighting the differences between the two techniques.

Roberts, L. W., Wilkinson, L., Peter, T., & Edgerton, J. (2015). *Understanding social statistics*. Don Mills: Oxford University Press (chapters 10–14). These chapters offer students the basic tools to examine the form and strength of bivariate relationships.

Multivariate Regression Analysis

9

Abstract

This final chapter provides an introduction into multivariate regression modeling. We will cover the logic behind multiple regression modeling and explain the interpretation of a multivariate regression model. We will further cover the assumptions this type of model is based upon. Finally, and using our data, we will provide concrete examples on how to interpret a multiple regression model.

9.1 The Logic Behind Multivariate Regression Analysis

Bivariate regression analysis is very rarely used in real applied research, because an outcome is hardly ever just dependent on one predictor. Rather, multiple factors normally explain the dependent variable (see Fig. 9.1). To highlight, if we want to explain a student's grade in an exam, several factors might come into play. A student's grade might depend on how much the respective student studied for the exam; it might depend on her health and even on her general mood. Multiple regression modeling allows us to absolutely and comparatively gauge the influence of all of these factors on the dependent variable.

Multiple regression analysis is an extension of bivariate regression analysis. It allows us to test the influence of multiple independent (predictor) variables on a dependent variable. Just like in the case of two variables, the goal of this method is to create an equation or a "model" that explains the impact of/relationship between these variables.

Let us assume that we want to explain the dependent variable "Y" and we have several independent variables $X_1 \ldots X_p$. Then, the multiple regression equation we need to calculate is:

© Springer International Publishing AG 2019
D. Stockemer, *Quantitative Methods for the Social Sciences*,
https://doi.org/10.1007/978-3-319-99118-4_9

Fig. 9.1 Predictors of a
student's grade

$$Y' = A + B_1X_1 + B_2X_2 + \ldots + B_pX_p$$

Y' is the predicted score of the dependent (criterion) variable (*dependent variable*).
A is a constant which gives the value of Y' when all Xs are zero (*Y-intercept or constant*).
Xs are all the independent variable values (*values of the independent variables*).
B_1–B_p are regression weights. They are the contribution of each *independent variable* to the predicted value of the dependent variable (i.e., each represents the change in Y' resulting from a *unit* change in a specific predictor variable *when all other predictors are held at constant values*).

Example Suppose we want to study the predictors of a student's grade in a math exam (see Figure 8.21). We ask a random sample of students at a German high school about their grade in their last math exam, the time they spent studying for this exam, their general mood, and whether they were in good perceived health when taking the exam. Let us further assume that we run a multiple regression model and receive the following equation (for now we ignore the question of whether the variables are statistically significant or not). We receive the following equation:

$$Y' = 10.5 + 3.1X_1 + 1.5X_2 + 0.5X_3 + e$$

We would interpret the model as follows:

10.5 (on a scale from 0 to 100) is the hypothetical grade a student is expected to get, if she does not study at all, her general health is at its worst (she would rank her health by the value 0), and her general mood is also at the lowest value (she would also rank this at 0).

3.1 is the slope coefficient for the variable study time. This implies that for every hour a student studies, her grade is expected to increase by 3.1 points.

1.5. is the slope coefficient for somebody's general health, indicating that per each point somebody's perceived health increases, her math grade is predicted to improve by 1.5 points.

0.5 is the slope coefficient for somebody's general mood. In other words, for each point somebody's general mood increases, her test performance is expected to increase by 0.5 points.

As we can see from the example, the multivariate regression model is an extension of the bivariate model. It has the same parameters and the interpretation is analogous. To do a multiple regression analysis in SPSS (or Stata), follow the same steps as you would follow for a bivariate regression. Just add more variables as independent variables.

9.2   The Functional Forms of Independent Variables to Include in a Multivariate Regression Model

In this introduction to survey research and quantitative methods, we only cover continuous dependent variables (noncontinuous dependent variables will be the subject of more advanced statistical courses). Yet, we still have to determine in what type of functional form we would include our independent variables. Provided that the relationship between a continuous independent and a continuous dependent variable is linear (the relationship follows a line), we will include the independent variables in its linear form. If a scatterplot would highlight that the relationship between independent and dependent variable is not linear (e.g., it follows a curve), we would need to transform the variable. However, this is also material for a more advanced class. We would also not change binary or dummy variables. The only variables we must be careful with, for the purpose of this introductory textbook, are categorical variables. If we have a categorical nominal variable (i.e., different religious affiliations), we create $N - 1$ dummy variables, with one of the categories serving as a reference category (see Table 4.14). If we have ordinal variables, we could also test whether the relationship is in fact ordered. For example, we could test via a multiple comparison test whether the relationship between times partying per week and money spent partying per week is in principle ordinal. By including the variable—times partying per week—in its linear ordinal form, we also assume that the relationship between partying less than one time per week and one time per week is the same as between four and five times per week. However, in the ANOVA or f-test, we find that this is not true (see Table 6.2). Rather, we find that students that party three times or less regardless of whether they party, on average, less than once, once, twice, or three times per week, spend approximately the same amount of money when they party; only students that party four or more times spend significantly more. Because of this dichotomy in the relationship, it would make sense to create a dummy variable between the two categories. (In the dataset, we label this variable money spent partying 3.)

9.3 Interpretation Help for a Multivariate Regression Model

When you want to interpret a multivariate regression model, we can follow the same logic as for a bivariate regression model. The four guiding steps can help:

1. Look at what variables are significant.
2. Interpret the substantive value of significant variable.
3. Compare the relative strength of the significant variables.
4. Interpret the model fit.

9.4 Doing a Multiple Regression Model in SPSS

In our sample survey, we have included seven possible predictor variables, and we want to determine the relative and absolute influence of these seven predictor variables on the dependent variable, money spent partying per week. Because we know from the ANOVA analysis (see Sect. 7.2.) that the relationship between the ordinal variable times partying and money spent partying is not linear, but rather only matters for individuals who party four times per week or more, we create a binary variable, coded 0 for partying three times or less per week and 1 for partying four times or more. We add this recoded independent variable together with the remaining six independent variables into the model (see Sect. 9.7) and label it Times_Partying_3. The dependent variable is money spent partying.

9.5 Interpreting a Multiple Regression Model in SPSS

Following the four steps outlined under Sect. 9.3., we can proceed as follows (see Table 9.1):

1. If we look at the significance level, we find that two variables are statistically significant (i.e., quality of extra-curricular activities and times partying 3). For all other variables, the significance level is higher than 0.05. Hence, we would conclude that these indicators do not influence the amount of money students spent per week partying.
2. The first significant variable, the quality of extra-curricular activities, has the expected negative sign indicating that the more the students enjoy their extra-curricular activities at their institution, the less money they spent weekly partying. This observation also confirms our initial hypothesis. Holding everything else constant, the model predicts that per every point a student enjoys her extra-curricular activities more, she spends 62 cents less per week partying.

Table 9.1 Multiple regression output in SPSS

Model Summary

Model	R	R Square	Adjusted R Square	Std. Error of the Estimate
1	.757[a]	.573	.480	21.74977

a. Predictors: (Constant), Times_Partying_3, Study_Time, Amount_Tuition_Student_Pays, Quality_Extra_Curricular_Activities, Gender, Year, Fun_Without_Alcohol

ANOVA[a]

Model		Sum of Squares	df	Mean Square	F	Sig.
1	Regression	20322.322	7	2903.189	6.137	.000[b]
	Residual	15137.678	32	473.052		
	Total	35460.000	39			

a. Dependent Variable: Money_Spent_Partying

b. Predictors: (Constant), Times_Partying_3, Study_Time, Amount_Tuition_Student_Pays, Quality_Extra_Curricular_Activities, Gender, Year, Fun_Without_Alcohol

Coefficients[a]

Model		Unstandardized Coefficients		Standardized Coefficients	t	Sig.
		B	Std. Error	Beta		
1	(Constant)	75.467	34.621		2.180	.037
	Study_Time	1.371	2.185	.141	.627	.535
	Gender	-3.316	8.290	-.056	-.400	.692
	Year	1.771	4.152	.065	.427	.673
	Fun_Without_Alcohol	-.058	.284	-.047	-.206	.838
	Quality_Extra_Curricular_Activities	-.588	.180	-.421	-3.272	.003
	Amount_Tuition_Student_Pays	.179	.119	.212	1.498	.144
	Times_Partying_3	26.641	10.373	.387	2.568	.015

a. Dependent Variable: Money_Spent_Partying

For example, this implies that somebody who thinks that the extra-curricular activities are very bad at her university (i.e., she rates the quality of extra-curricular activities at 0) spends 62 dollars more per week studying than somebody who thinks that the extra-curricular activities are excellent (i.e., she rates the quality of extra-curricular activities at 100).

The second significant variable, times partying 3, also has the expected positive sign. The regression coefficient of 24.81 indicates that people that party four or more times are expected to spend nearly 25 dollars more on their partying habits than students that party three times or less.

3. If we compare the two statistically significant variables, we find that the standardized beta coefficient is higher for the variable quality of extra-curricular activities (i.e., the standardized beta coefficient is –0.421) than for the variable times partying 3 (0.387). This higher standard beta coefficient illustrates that the variable quality of extra-curricular activities has more explanatory power in the model than the variable times partying 3.
4. The model fits the data quite well; the seven independent variables explain 57% of the variance in the dependent variable, the amount of money students spent partying. (The R-squared is 0.568.)

9.6 Doing a Multiple Regression Model in Stata

In our survey, we have included seven possible predictor variables, and we want to determine the relative and absolute influence of these seven predictor variables on the dependent variable. Because we know from the ANOVA analysis (see Table 6.2) that the relationship between the ordinal variable times partying and money spent partying is not linear but rather only becomes different for individuals who party four times or more, we create a binary variable, coded 0 for partying three times or less per week and 1 for partying four times or more. We add this recoded independent variable together with the remaining six independent variables into the model (see Sect. 9.8). The dependent variable is money spent partying.

9.7 Interpreting a Multiple Regression Model in Stata

Following the four steps outlined under 10.3., we can proceed as follows (see Tables 9.2 and 9.3):

Table 9.2 Multiple regression output in Stata

Source	SS	df	MS			
				Number of obs	=	40
				F(7, 32)	=	6.14
Model	20322.3215	7	2903.18879	Prob > F	=	0.0001
Residual	15137.6785	32	473.052452	R-squared	=	0.5731
				Adj R-squared	=	0.4797
Total	35460	39	909.230769	Root MSE	=	21.75

Money_Spent_Partying	Coef.	Std. Err.	t	P>|t|	[95% Conf. Interval]	
Study_Time	1.370689	2.184869	0.63	0.535	-3.079744	5.821122
Gender	-3.316106	8.290119	-0.40	0.692	-20.20253	13.57031
Year	1.771348	4.152033	0.43	0.673	-6.686067	10.22876
Fun_Without_Alcohol	-.0583414	.2836462	-0.21	0.838	-.6361098	.519427
Quality_Extra_Curricular_Activ	-.5883588	.1798321	-3.27	0.003	-.9546649	-.2220527
Amount_Tuition_Student_Pays	.1788863	.1194251	1.50	0.144	-.0643748	.4221473
Times_Partying_3	26.6411	10.3729	2.57	0.015	5.512191	47.77
_cons	75.46679	34.62063	2.18	0.037	4.946871	145.9867

Table 9.3 Multiple regression output in Stata with standardized coefficients

Source	SS	df	MS		
				Number of obs =	40
				F(7, 32) =	6.14
Model	20322.3215	7	2903.18879	Prob > F =	0.0000
Residual	15137.6785	32	473.052452	R-squared =	0.5731
				Adj R-squared =	0.4797
Total	35460	39	909.230769	Root MSE =	21.75

Money_Spent_Partying	Coef.	Std. Err.	t	P>|t|	Beta
Study_Time	1.370689	2.184869	0.63	0.535	.1406508
Gender	-3.316106	8.290119	-0.40	0.692	-.055618
Year	1.771348	4.152033	0.43	0.673	.0654421
Fun_Without_Alcohol	-.0583414	.2836462	-0.21	0.838	-.04718
Quality_Extra_Curricular_Activ	-.5883588	.1798321	-3.27	0.003	-.4212501
Amount_Tuition_Student_Pays	.1788863	.1194251	1.50	0.144	.2120732
Times_Partying_3	26.6411	10.3729	2.57	0.015	.387448
_cons	75.46679	34.62063	2.18	0.037	.

1. If we look at the significance level, we find that two variables are statistically significant (i.e., quality of extra-curricular activities and times partying 3). For all other variables, the significance level is higher than 0.05. Hence, we would conclude that these indicators do not influence the amount of money students spent per week partying.

2. The first significant variable, the quality of extra-curricular activities, has the expected negative sign indicating that the more students enjoy their extra-curricular activities at their institution, the less money they spent weekly partying. This observation also confirms our initial hypothesis. Holding everything else constant, the model predicts that per every point a student enjoys her extra-curricular activities more, she spends 62 cents less per week partying. For example, this implies that somebody who thinks that the extra-curricular activities are very bad at her university (i.e., she rates the quality of extra-curricular activities at 0) spends 62 dollars more per week studying than somebody who thinks that the extra-curricular activities are excellent (i.e., she rates the quality of extra-curricular activities at 100).

   The second significant variable, times partying 2, also has the expected positive sign. The regression coefficient of 24.81 indicates that people that party four or more times are expected to spend nearly 25 dollars more on their weekly partying habits than students that party three times or less.

3. If we compare the two statistically significant variables, we find that the standardized beta coefficient is higher for the variable quality of extra-curricular activities (i.e., the standardized beta coefficient is –0.421) than for the variable times partying 3 (0.387). This higher standard beta coefficient illustrates that the variable quality of extra-curricular activities has more explanatory power in the model than the variable times partying 3.

4. The model fits the data quite well; the seven independent variables explain nearly 57% of the variance in the dependent variable, the amount of money students spent partying. (The R-squared is 0.573.)

9.8   Reporting the Results of a Multiple Regression Analysis

In the multiple regression analysis (see Table 9.2), we evaluated the influence of seven independent variables (the quality of extra-curricular activities, students' study time per week, the year students are in, gender, whether they party two times or less or three times or more per week, the degree to which they think that they can have fun without alcohol, and the amount of tuition the students pay) on the dependent variable, the weekly amount of money students spent partying. We find that two of the seven variables are statistically significant and show the expected effect; that is, the more students think that the extra-curriculars at their university are good, the less money they spent partying per week. The same applies to students that party few times; they too spend less money going out. In substantive terms, the model predicts that per every point students increase their ranking of the extra-curricular activities at their school, they will spend 59 cents less partying per week. The coefficient for the dummy variable, partying two times or less or three times or more per week, indicates that students that party three or more times are predicted to spend 26 dollars more on their partying habits than students that party less. Using the 95% benchmark, none of the other variables is statistically significant. Consequently, we cannot interpret the other coefficients because they are not different from zero. In terms of model fit, the data fits the model fairly well: the seven independent variables explain 57% of the variance in the dependent variable.

9.9   Finding the Best Model

In real research the inclusion of variables into a regression model should be theoretically driven; that is, theory should tell us which independent variables we should include in a model to explain and predict a dependent variable. However, we might also be interested in finding the best model. There are two ways to proceed, and there is some disagreement among statisticians: One way is to only include statistically significant variables into the model. Another way is to use the adjusted R-squared as a benchmark. To recall, the adjusted R-squared is a measure of model fit that allows us to compare different models. For every additional predictor I include in the model, the adjusted R-squared increases only if the new term improves the model beyond pure chance. (Please note that a poor predictor can decrease the adjusted R-squared, but it can never decrease the R-squared.) Using the adjusted R-squared as a benchmark to find the best model, we should proceed as follows: (1) start with the complete model, which includes all the predictors, (2) remove the non-statistically significant predictor with the lowest standardized coefficient, and (3) continue this procedure until the

Table 9.4 Finding the best model

	Model 1	Model 2	Model 3	**Model 4**	Model 5
Quality of extra-curricular activities	–0.421	–0.415	–0.416	**0.421**	–0.442
Gender	0.056	0.062	0.051		
Study time per week	0.141	0.200	0.159	**0.140**	
Year of study	0.065	0.051			
Times partying (two times or less/ three times or more	0.387	0.401	0.421	**0.418**	0.418
Fun without alcohol	–0.047				
Amount of tuition student pays	0.179	0.218	0.201	**0.180**	0.150
Constant	75.47	70.22	76.36	**77.53**	92.66
R-squared	0.5731	0.5725	0.5707	**56.87**	0.5502
Adjusted R-squared	0.4797	0.4948	0.5075	**51.94**	0.5127

adjusted R-squared does no longer increases. Table 9.4 highlights this procedure. We start with the full model. The full model has an adjusted R-squared of 0.4797. We take out the variable with the lowed standardized beta coefficient (fun without alcohol). After taking out this variable, we see that the adjusted R-squared increases to 0.4948 (see Model 2). This indicates that the variable fun without alcohol does not add anything substantial to the model and should be removed. In a next step, we remove the variable, year of study. Removing this variable leads to another increase in the adjusted R-squared (i.e., the new adjusted R-squared is 0.5075), indicating again that this variable does not add anything substantively to the model and should be removed (see Model 3). Next, we remove the variable gender and see another increase in the adjusted R-squared to 0.5194. If we now remove the variable with the lowest adjusted R-squared, the study time per week, we find that the adjusted R-squared decreases to 0.5127 (see Model 5), which is lower than the adjusted R-squared from Model 4, which is 0.5114. Based on these calculations, we can conclude that Model 4 has the best model fit.

9.10   Assumptions of the Classical Linear Regression Model or Ordinary Least Square Regression Model (OLS)

The classical linear regression model (OLS) is the simplest type of regression model. OLS only works with a continuous dependent variable. It has ten underlying assumptions:

1. **Linearity in the parameters**: Linearity in the parameters implies that the relationship between a continuous independent variable and a dependent variable must roughly follow a line. Relationships that do not follow a line (e.g., they might follow a quadratic function or a logarithmic function) must be included into the model using the correct functional forms (more advanced textbooks in regression analysis will capture these cases).

2. **X is fixed**: This rule implies that one observation can only have one x and one y value.

3. **Mean of disturbance is zero**: This follows the rule to draw the ordinary least square line. We draw the best fitting line, which implies that the summed up distance of the points below the line is the same as the summed up distance above the line.

4. **Homoscedasticity:** The homoscedasticity assumption implies that the variance around the regression line is similar for all the predictor variables around the regression line (X) (see Fig. 9.2). To highlight, in the first graph, the points are distributed rather equally around a hypothetical line. In the second graph, the points are closer to the hypothetical line at the bottom of the graph in comparison to the top of the graph. In our example, the first graph would be an example of homoscedasticity and the second graph an example of data suffering from heteroscedasticity. At this stage in your learning, it is important that you have heard about heteroscedasticity, but details of the problem will be covered in more advanced textbooks and classes.

5. **No autocorrelation:** There are basically two forms of autocorrelation: (1) contemporaneous correlation, where the dependent variable from one observations affects the dependent variable of another observation in the same dataset (e.g., Mexican growth rates might not be independent because growth rates in the United States might affect growth rates in Mexico), and (2) autocorrelation in pooled time series datasets. That is, past values of the dependent variable influence future values of the dependent (e.g., the US growth rate in 2017 might affect the US growth rate in 2018). This second type of autocorrelation is not really pertinent for cross-sectional analysis but becomes relevant for panel analysis.

6. **No endogeneity:** Endogeneity is one of the fundamental problems in regression analysis. Regression analysis is based on the assumption that the independent variable impacts the dependent variable but not vice versa. In many real-world political science scenarios, this assumption is problematic. For example, there is debate in the literature whether high women's representation in instances of power influences/decreases corruption or whether low levels of corruption foster the election of women (see Esarey and Schwindt-Bayer 2017). There are statistical remedies such as instrumental regression techniques, which can model a feedback loop, that is, more advanced techniques can measure whether two variables influence themselves mutually. These techniques will also be covered in more advanced books and classes.

7. **No omitted variables:** We have an omitted variable problem if we do not include a variable in our regression model that theory tells us that we should include. Omitting a relevant or important variable from a model can have four negative consequences: (1) If the omitted variable is correlated with the included variables, then the parameters estimated in the model are biased, meaning that their expected values do not match their true values. (2) The error variance of the estimated parameters is biased. (3) The confidence intervals of included variables and more general the hypothesis testing procedures are unreliable, and (4) the R-squared of the estimated model is unreliable.

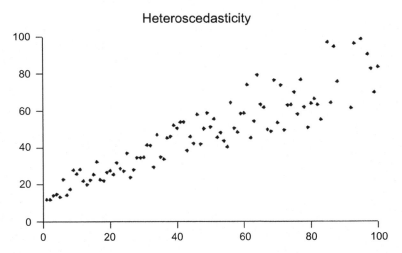

Fig. 9.2 Homoscedasticity and heteroscedasticity

8. **More cases than parameters ($N > k$):** Technically, a regression analysis only
   runs if we have more cases than parameters. In more general terms, the regression estimates become more reliable the more cases we have.
9. **No constant "variables":** For an independent variable to explain variation in a
   dependent variable, there must be variation in the independent variable. If there is
   no variation, then there is no reason to include the independent variable in a

regression model. The same applies to the dependent variable. If the dependent variable is constant or near constant, and does not vary with independent variables, then there is no reason to conduct any analysis in the first place.

10. **No perfect collinearity among regressors**: This rule means that the independent variables included in a regression should represent different concepts. To highlight, the more two variables are correlated, the more they will take explanatory power from each other (if they are perfectly collinear, a regression program such as Stata or SPSS cannot distinguish these variables from one another). This becomes problematic because relevant variables might become nonsignificant in a regression model, if they are too highly correlated with other relevant variables. More advanced books and classes will also tackle the problem of perfect collinearity and multicollinearity. For the purposes of an introductory course, it is enough if you have heard about multicollinearity.

Reference

Esarey, J., & Schwindt-Bayer, L. A. (2017). Women's representation, accountability and corruption in democracies. *British Journal of Political Science*, 1–32.

Further Reading

Since basically all books listed under bivariate correlation and regression analysis also cover multiple regression analysis, the books I present here go beyond the scope of this textbook here. These books could be interesting further reads, in particular to students, who want to learn more what is covered here.

Heeringa, S. G., West, B. T., & Berglund, P. A. (2017). *Applied survey data analysis*. Boca Raton: Chapman and Hall/CRC. An overview of different approaches to analyze complex sample survey data. In addition to multiple linear regression analysis the topics covered include different types of maximum likelihood estimations such as logit, probit, and ordinal regression analysis, as well as survival or event history analysis.

Lewis-Beck, C., & Lewis-Beck, M. (2015). *Applied regression: An introduction* (Vol. 22). Thousand Oaks: Sage A comprehensive introduction into different types of regression techniques.

Pesaran, M. H. (2015). *Time series and panel data econometrics*. Oxford: Oxford University Press. Comprehensive introduction into different forms of time series models and panel data estimations.

Wooldridge, J. M. (2015). *Introductory econometrics: A modern approach*. Mason, OH: Nelson Education. Comprehensive book about various regression techniques; it is, however, mathematically relatively advanced.

Appendix 1: The Data of the Sample Questionnaire

	MSP	ST	Gender	Year	TP	FWA	QECA	ATSP
Student 1	50	7	0	2	2	60	90	30
Student 2	35	8	1	3	1	70	40	50
Student 3	120	12	1	3	4	30	20	60
Student 4	80	3	0	4	4	50	50	100
Student 5	100	11	0	1	1	30	10	0
Student 6	120	14	1	5	4	20	20	0
Student 7	90	11	0	4	2	50	50	0
Student 8	80	10	1	4	3	40	50	10
Student 9	70	9	0	3	3	30	50	60
Student 10	80	8	1	2	3	40	40	100
Student 11	60	12	1	4	2	60	40	0
Student 12	50	14	1	2	1	30	70	10
Student 13	100	13	0	3	4	0	30	0
Student 14	90	15	0	3	0	0	20	0
Student 15	60	7	0	3	3	60	50	0
Student 16	40	6	1	4	0	70	90	0
Student 17	60	5	1	4	2	80	50	60
Student 18	90	8	0	5	2	90	30	70
Student 19	130	12	1	4	5	10	20	50
Student 20	70	11	0	1	1	20	60	30
Student 21	80	13	1	3	4	10	70	50
Student 22	50	6	0	4	4	60	40	10
Student 23	110	5	1	4	4	70	30	100
Student 24	60	8	1	2	3	50	60	100
Student 25	70	10	1	4	2	60	40	80
Student 26	60	10	1	4	2	40	70	10
Student 27	50	11	0	3	2	30	50	0
Student 28	75	4	0	4	3	80	70	0
Student 29	80	7	0	6	4	90	30	0
Student 30	30	12	1	3	0	20	80	40
Student 31	70	7	0	4	3	70	30	10
Student 32	70	14	1	2	1	0	50	100

(continued)

© Springer International Publishing AG 2019
D. Stockemer, *Quantitative Methods for the Social Sciences*,
https://doi.org/10.1007/978-3-319-99118-4

	MSP	ST	Gender	Year	TP	FWA	QECA	ATSP
Student 33	70	3	0	4	3	60	40	50
Student 34	60	11	1	4	2	50	50	70
Student 35	70	9	0	2	1	60	20	40
Student 36	60	11	0	3	1	20	60	60
Student 37	60	11	1	4	1	30	40	20
Student 38	90	8	1	1	2	50	10	50
Student 39	70	9	0	3	3	50	90	30
Student 40	200	10	1	4	5	40	20	100

MSP Money spent partying, *ST* Study time, *Gender* Gender, *Year* Year, *TS* Times spent parting per week, *FWA* Fun without alcohol, *QECA* Quality of extra curricula activities, *ATSP* Amount of tuition the student pays

Appendix 2: Possible Group Assignments That Go with This Course

As an optional component, this book is built around a practical assignment. The assignment consists of a semester-long group project, which gives students the opportunity to practically apply their quantitative research skills. In more detail, at the beginning of the term, students are assigned to a study/ working group that consists of four individuals. Over the course of the semester, each group is expected to draft an original questionnaire, solicit 40 respondents of their survey (i.e. 10 per student) and perform a set of exercises with their data (i.e. some exercises on descriptive statistics, means testing/ correlation and regression analysis).

Assignment 1:
Go together in groups of four to five people and design your own questionnaire. It should include continuous, dummy and categorical variables (after Chap. 4).

Assignment 2:
Each group member should collect ten surveys based on a convenience sample. Because of time constraints there is no need to conduct a pre-test of the survey.

Assignment 3:
Conduct some descriptive statistics with some of your variables. Also construct a Pie Chart, Boxplot and Histogram.

Assignment 4:
Your assignment will consist of a number of data exercises

1. Graph your dependent variable as a histogram
2. Graph your dependent variable and one continuous independent variable as a boxplot
3. Display some descriptive statistics
4. Conduct an independent samples t-test. Use the dependent variable of your study; as grouping variable use your dichotomous variable (or one of your dichotomous variables).
5. Conduct a one way anova test. Use the dependent variable of your study; As factor use one of your ordinal variables

© Springer International Publishing AG 2019
D. Stockemer, *Quantitative Methods for the Social Sciences*,
https://doi.org/10.1007/978-3-319-99118-4

6. Run a correlation matrix with your dependent variable and two other continuous variables.
7. Run a multivariate regression analysis with all your independent variables and your dependent variable.

Index

© Springer International Publishing AG 2019
D. Stockemer, *Quantitative Methods for the Social Sciences*,
https://doi.org/10.1007/978-3-319-99118-4

Printed by Printforce, the Netherlands